Modern Cabins

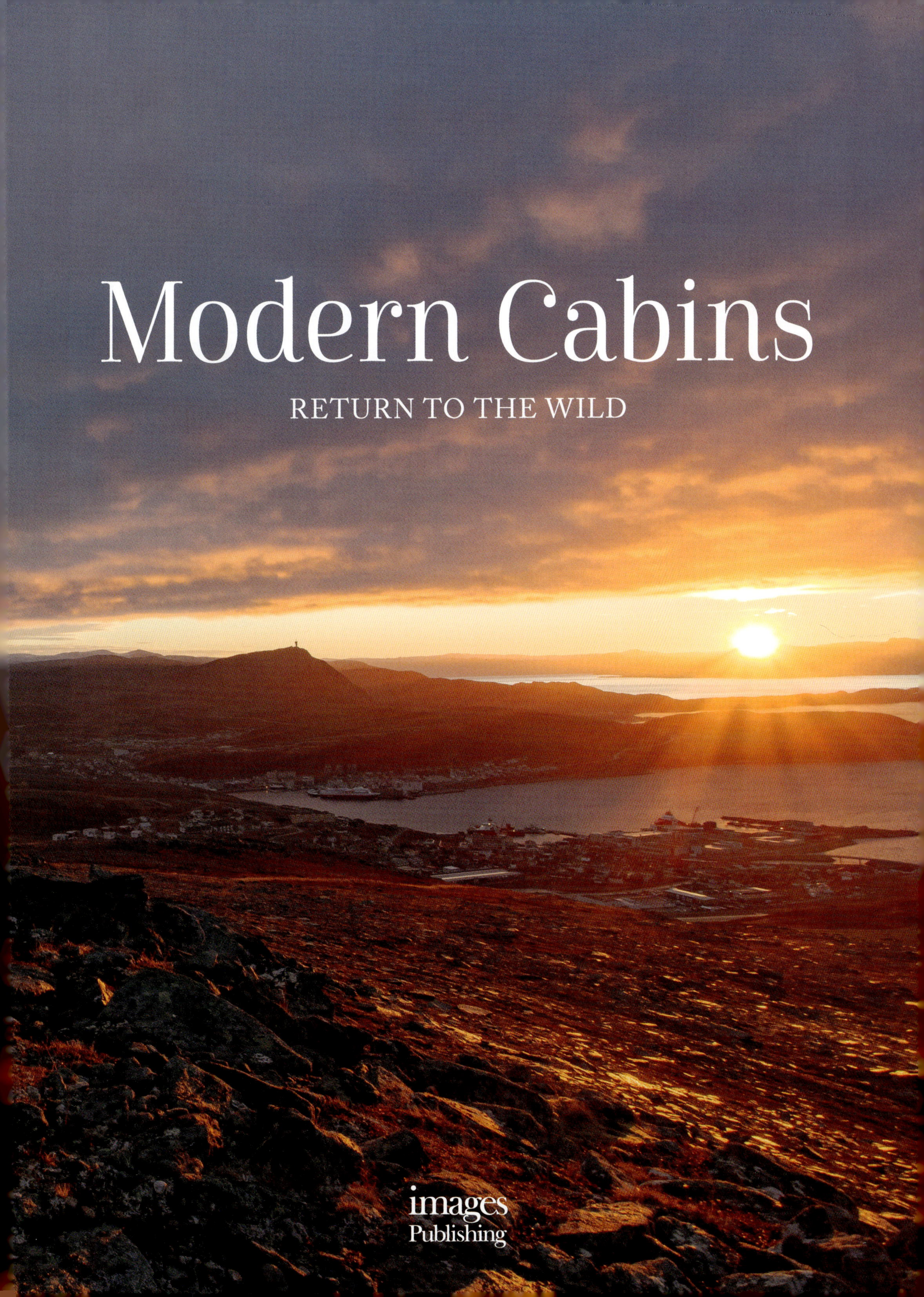

Modern Cabins

RETURN TO THE WILD

images Publishing

Contents

Introduction

By Dev Desai

I have always been a city dweller. This means, having become accustomed to the continual din of traffic and construction on the street; to the air-conditioned and sterile spaces that block off the world outside; and to the fast-paced life in the metropolis, where one rarely has the opportunity to sit still and reflect on grand notions like "existence" and "purpose."

I distinctly remember my first visit to a site in Bettagere Estate in Coorg, India, a few years ago for a project with an unusual brief: a space for solitude immersed in nature, yet equipped with all the modern amenities for a comfortable living experience. "Not the typical brief," I thought, but as I walked through the area set in the mountain range of Suntikoopa, the brief's requirements began to resonate and make complete sense. My visit to that site was an experience so pure, it would, in the coming days, have a profound impact on me, and, in the years to come, shape the direction the studio would take.

The experience in the forest that day in Coorg was a temple of sensation that delighted the mind, body, and soul: the rustling of leaves in the cool winter breeze, the crackling of twigs under my feet, and the birds chirping high above me were scenes I would not soon forget. The sensation of the warm dappled light that speckled through the tree canopy offered relief from the cold and dew, as did the crisp air that filled my lungs, a refreshing change from the city's heavy, smoggy atmosphere that I'd come to accept as just another normal day. The odor from the wet earth and the aroma of the coffee beans from the distant roastery starting its day offered a stimulating blend; and the absence of car horns and the city's incessant chatter harmonized a sort of poetic silence that places faith in one's capacity for introspection and self-healing.

Modern Cabins: Return to the Wild celebrates our primordial connection with nature through a compilation of stunning contemporary architectural interventions in pristine natural settings, each as diverse as the countries and landscapes in which they are built. Cabins continue to prove their popularity as we collectively dream of escaping into nature, *with* nature, away from global troubles. In a post-pandemic world that is ever more digitally connected, and especially with spaces of living and working in this world becoming synonymous with each other, we are all the more fervently guided toward this yearning, seeking an escape to nature that is not just a dream, but also a very achievable reality. This follow-up to the popular *Cabins: Escape to Nature* provides a new raft of intriguing cabin designs set in beautiful landscapes, revealing that that this idealized way of life (or rather, time-out from the day-to-day grind of life) is one that is gaining tremendous traction, not only for the connection to nature that it bestows, but also for its novel "vacation locally" aspect.

This second book showcases a spectacular compilation of contemporary cabins situated in a variety of natural settings that are categorized according to environmental contexts, such as forests and mountains, and waterside and rural locations. Against these inspiring and stunning backdrops, it features projects that extend from luxurious accommodations to the increasingly popular modular and prefabricated cabin models designed for fuss-free off-grid living—each cabin different, but all cued to only one purpose: escape.

As these projects attest, the key ingredients for great cabin design stem from the relationship between person, the natural context, and the cabin that encapsulates the lifestyle of the occupant while paying homage to its surroundings. Each cabin exudes a romantic relationship with nature through carefully curated experiences, and by engaging the senses—whether it be through the emphasis on the visual axis, such as in Atelier Marko Brajovic's Bow House, which celebrates the views between mango trees; or like in Forest Glamp by Bourgeois / Lechasseur architectes, through seamlessly blending into its natural context with reflective glazing, while visually connecting every internal space with the outdoors.

Some cabins also engage the inhabitant through a wide array of textures and materials, as exemplified by the very elegant and contemporary Koto Muutama Cabin by KOTO Design, as well as by Niliaitta by Studio Puisto Architects, which celebrates the age-old Japanese technique of burnt cedar cladding known as *shou sugi ban* on the exterior, while featuring subtle interiors that frame the views.

The contemporary cabins showcased in this book aspire to be so much more than mere functional shelters in the forest, the mountains, or the vast outdoors. They personify within their elegant forms the choice of materials and method of construction, the aspiration of the designer and the dweller, the sensitivity to and respect for the natural context, and the ability to cater to modern comforts and lifestyles. However, materializing the concepts to realize the many possibilities that cabins can be is not without struggle. My experience in India came to show that one of the key challenges associated with realizing the architectural vision for cabins in pristine natural settings is more often than not a logistical one. Poor vehicular accessibility and lack of on-site resources for construction can sometimes throw a wrench in the works. A renewed awareness for sustainability, has also called for tremendous explorations in modular, pre-fabricated, and innovative solutions for construction, as well as the use of recyclable materials.

Cabin Moss by Béres Architects epitomizes respect for its natural context beautifully, with its innovative foundation system that seeks to cohabit with its context instead of impinging on it. HANNAH's Ashen Cabin looks to the future of rural constructions by advancing the use of technologies, such as robotics and 3D printing in timber and concrete construction, veering away from the conventional panel and module-based prefabrication system.

From the complex and sophisticated Mountaineer's Refuge by Gonzalo Iturriaga Arquitectos that curates the dweller's experience through its multifold structure, to the simple, yet cozy Filmmaker's Hut by Pirinen Salo Oy, built as a small shingle-clad workspace on the shore of Lake Porovesi, Finland, the cabin projects in this book are exemplary examples of architectural interventions in natural landscapes. They captivate the soul and tap into the innate connection between self and nature, enabling one to embark upon a mystical journey of self-discovery, as only nature and its marvels can extend.

Dev Desai founded DDAA (Dev Desai Architects and Associates) in late 2020. His formative development as an architect was molded under the guidance of Pritzker Laureate Toyo Ito & Associates, Architects (Japan) and Vo Trong Nghia Architects (Vietnam). Both continue to have a strong influence on his work.

As a young and dynamic studio, DDAA constantly challenges the threshold of architectural design through a contemporary unique language. One of their initial projects was the design and development of a tiny cabin on a coffee estate, as an alternative way of living during the recent pandemic. To minimize the ecological impact, the cabin was prefabricated and assembled within four weeks. What started out as a humble architectural project has now evolved into a specialization in such constructions, with projects in the United States, Europe, and the Middle East, along with several projects in India set amid pristine natural settings.

Dev Desai also founded Re-Build, a research venture that addresses the challenges in conventional prefabrication that aims to merge the power of digital fabrication to amortize the cost of construction, reduce dependency on manual labor, eliminate the need for heavy machinery, and reduce assembly time to a few days.

The connection with nature and the desire to push the boundaries of architecture and construction are the guiding principles behind his work.

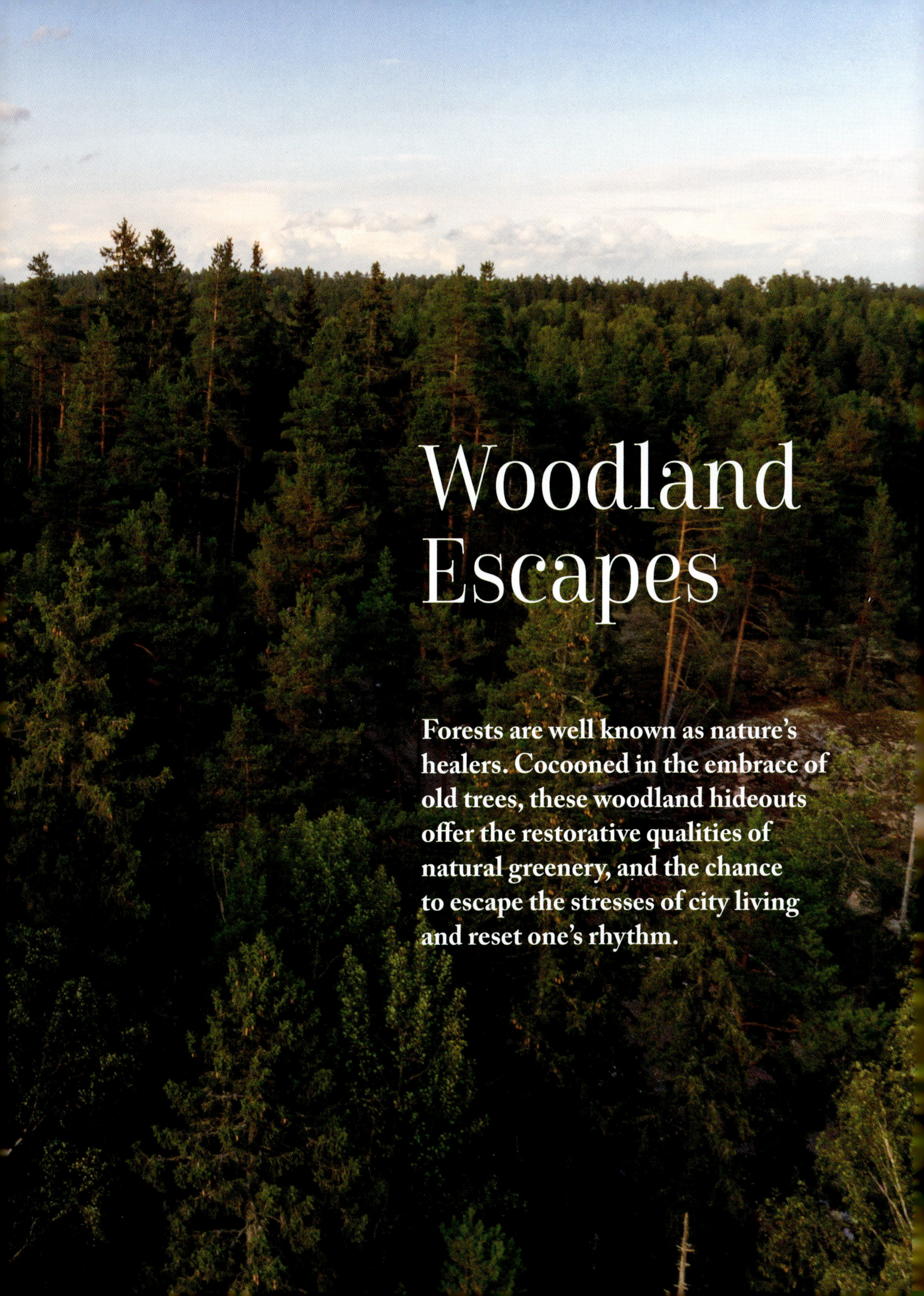

Woodland Escapes

Forests are well known as nature's healers. Cocooned in the embrace of old trees, these woodland hideouts offer the restorative qualities of natural greenery, and the chance to escape the stresses of city living and reset one's rhythm.

Sitting Pretty

Designed as a modular system, this cabin is tailored to be constructed in a workshop first and transported whole. The structure is defined as a set of individual elements, such as columns, floors, walls, and roof, which allows different sizes and configurations of the building.

As the final site is always a variable, with the only known factors being the elements, the roof of the cabin is designed to protect the structure from the sun's heat. It appears like it's floating in the wind, and is shaped to collect rainwater, trickling it down from one plane to another. Standing on slender legs, which are equipped with variable height adjustments, the cabin is thoughtfully planned to adapt to its natural terrain. The metal used in the construction and façade is non-colored and marked with a unique pattern that is created during its manufacturing process. This embellishes each cabin with different façade graphics. Within its metal shell is a warm, natural plywood finish.

The cabin's first constructed model on Apple Island—a lake island in Lithuania featuring exceptional natural surroundings, characteristic terrain, and lush native trees—highlights the advantages of its architecture. Requiring minimal construction works, the site embraces the visually light volume of the building, blending it harmoniously into the natural landscape. The program arranges two double bedrooms, a living room, kitchen, and bathroom. This extensive function is made possible by transformable furniture. A folding glass door opens fully to extend the interior to an outdoor terrace overlooking the lake.

019 CABIN (2020), Apple Island, Lithuania

Nothing to Waste

Ashen Cabin is a dual-solution architecture, solving a critical environmental problem close to home, while also providing an escape into nature.

In the summer of 2002, the Emerald Ash Borer beetle was unintentionally introduced to forests in America via human trade and travel. With a voracious appetite, it has come to threaten almost nine billion trees across the United States, and nearly one in ten ash trees in New York.

Rather than discard and burn compromised ash trees (considered a specific form of waste material), which would release CO_2 into the atmosphere, Ashen Cabin uses them as a material resource in its construction, with the help of robotics and 3D printing technology. This strategy binds carbon to the earth and offsets the harvesting of other commonly used wood species; it also presents as a new approach to sustainable housing design, development, and construction in the United States, and possibly beyond.

Previously, mature ash trees compromised by the industrious beetle could not be used as a source of lumber for home construction because of their irregular geometries. But robotic technology makes it possible to process irregular ash trees, using 3D scans as a basis for translating and digitizing the trees' complex, irregular geometries.

To further reduce CO_2 emissions, the use of concrete is minimized in the cabin and applied only when structurally needed through 3D printing, which eliminates the need for "wasteful" formwork.

ASHEN CABIN (2019), Ithaca, New York, United States

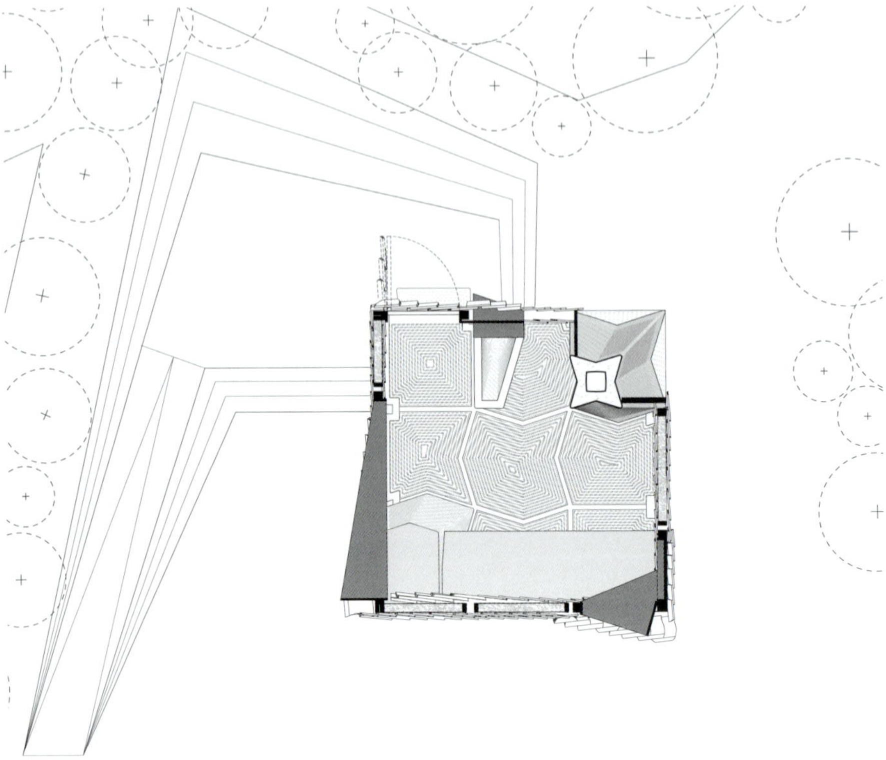

Floor plan

Floating Hideaway

Cabin Moss was built to simple priorities: respect the site and context, stay small, help the environment, and maintain privacy. And it does so without compromising comfortable living or interior style.

Among 100-year-old gigantic trees in an untouched forest in Alpokalja, Hungary, the cabin rests on thin stilts to protect the roots of the trees, as well as to avoid ground excavations during construction, which would have ruined the landscape. This smart foundation materializes on the principle of "measure twice, dig once," and a purposefully planned structural system.

Floating above a sloping terrain, this small forest hideaway projects a simple form that turns it back on its few neighbors to angle windows and openings toward an endless forest view. A cross section with two right angles facing each other creates great visual contacts with the surrounding landscape, while also allowing taller windows—which are given special attention to double as adornments on the façade. In a playful game of mimicry, they reflect the forest scenery and add dynamism to the single-material façade, as they blend the cabin into the green backdrop.

The subtle exterior is contrasted with a warm and cozy interior that is completed by timber finishes and an expansive view of the surrounding greenery. The layout is particular and creates no unnecessary spaces, nor does it waste precious square feet, in order to maintain a small footprint. This was just the starting point of being environmentally friendly; it also has high-end building materials, a well-designed insulation system, a meticulous design, and an exceptional microclimate to keep power consumption low and allow a comfortable and sustainable way of life.

CABIN MOSS (2021), Kőszeg, Hungary

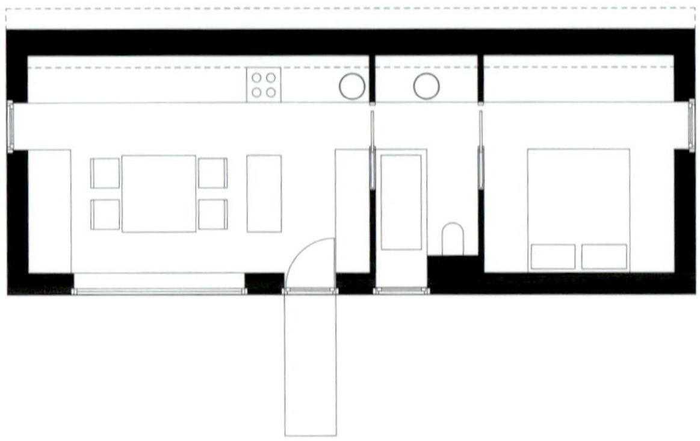

Floor plan

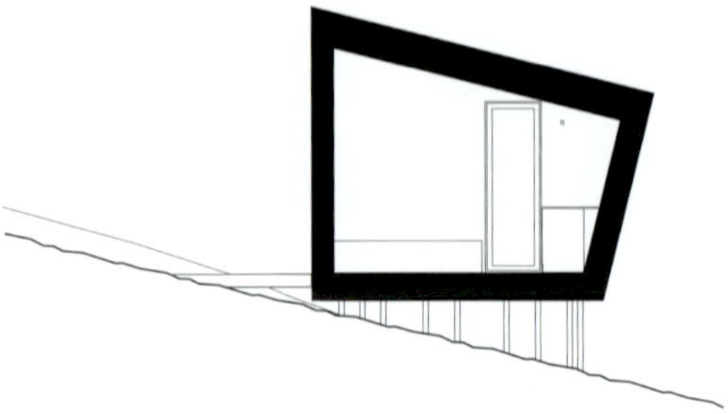

Cross section

Perched for the View

On a seemingly treacherous and unbuildable site, a mountain-side cabin takes position as a weekend retreat for a family of four. The site, set in White Mountains, New England, United States, known for rugged granite outcroppings, was discovered on a scouting hike and inspired unconventional design solutions to make the cabin a reality.

The cabin perches on one such granite outcropping, projecting precariously over a steep drop-off to afford dramatic eastern views across the valley below. The site drove the design—as the family grew from two to four over the course of the design process, it was essential to maximize the build area and the cabin's footprint. Instead of leveling the granite ledge, the topography is embraced; the structure is lifted on nine hand-poured concrete footings so that the structure treads lightly on the sloped site. Minimal trees were cleared, just enough to provide specific views of the stunning mountain peaks through a full-width, sliding glass window-wall.

To shorten construction time and reduce disturbance to the site, all parts of the wood framing were engineered, CNC-cut, and delivered to the site, labeled and ready to be assembled.

Prefabrication techniques allowed the freedom to explore complex geometries in wood framing; this was then clad with standing seam aluminum panels, tongue-and-groove cedar boards, and folded stainless-steel sheets in various spaces. Shaped by its surroundings, this mountain retreat makes a lasting connection between what is there and what is to come.

CABIN ON A ROCK (2017), White Mountains, New Hampshire, United States

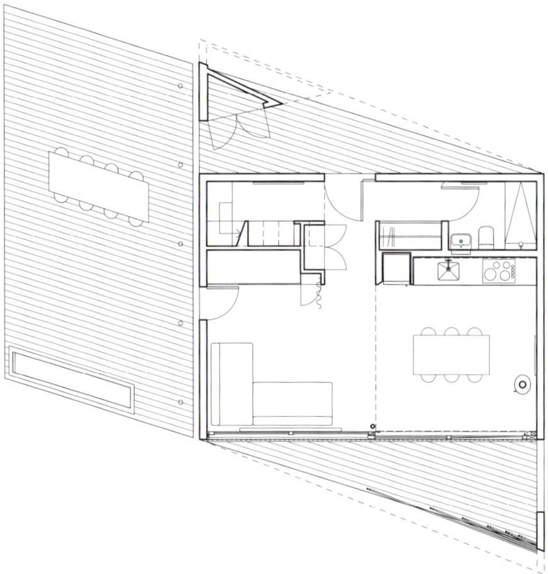

First floor plan

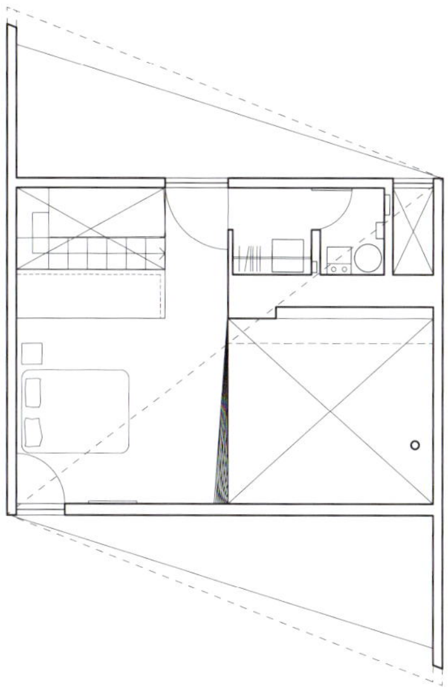

Second floor plan

A Woven Dream

Casa Tejida, or Woven House, is set in a rural community in the municipality of Nocaima in Cundinamarca, Colombia. The challenging access routes to the area limit visitors, which has allowed wildlife and nature to thrive, creating a rich biodiversity.

The architecture relates to the environment and context in which it has been developed—through its physical form and building techniques. It is located perpendicular to contour lines—in contrast with local constructions—to adapt better to the topography and avoid large earthworks. Pre-Hispanic architecture inspires the repetitive wood structure; some columns are buried in the ground while others rest on stones. This concept is based on the idea that the wooden pillars hold the house in its early years, but as they age and rot, the columns resting on the stones will eventually hold the bearing load. The woven exterior is a result of collaboration with a local weaver to adapt intricate weave overlaps as a construction element.

Serving as a prototype of a construction that highlights techniques and materials better adapted to the places and climates they are located in, Casa Tejida is a low-impact high-quality solution that creates a healthy, better ventilated, and more livable environment. Reducing the constructed area, eliminating corridors and transitional spaces, and designing a wooden floor that maximizes living space all combine to use fewer materials and create a smaller build area.

CASA TEJIDA (WOVEN HOUSE) (2019), Cundinamarca, Colombia

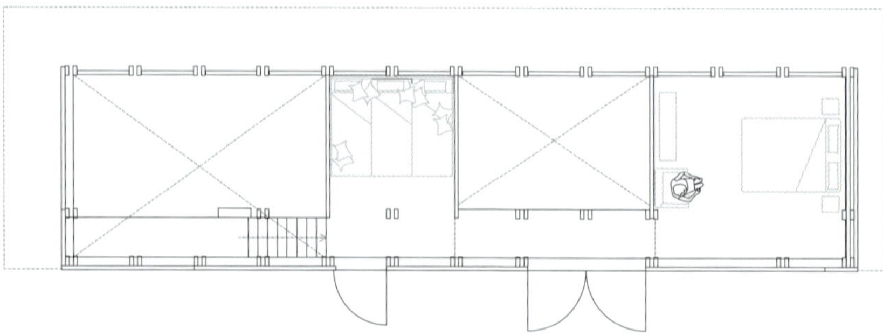

Second-floor plan

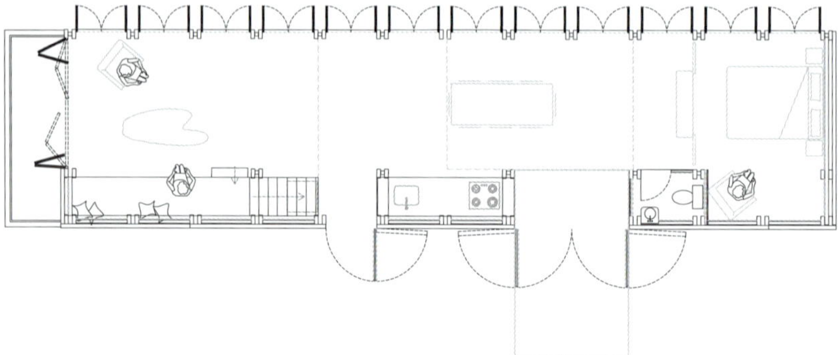

First-floor plan

Peaceful Reflections

This cabin, an urban interpretation of living wild, is situated close to one of Québec's most popular ski resorts, Massif Petite-Rivière-Saint-François. It dazzles with twice the views of its beautiful surroundings, with a reflective glazed façade that helps the cabin disappear into the trees. Darkened exterior wood slat cladding is interspersed with the glass to reinforce this sense of immersion and connection.

The dark tone on the outside carries through into the interior, and is set off by a pine ceiling. Designed for up to six people, the layout accommodates a cozy living and dining area—complete with a fireplace—a bathroom, an outdoor spa, and two enclosed bedrooms. Windows at every turn possible extend the beautiful greenery right up to the door, the living room, the bedroom, and even the kitchen, to encourage an intimate experience with nature. To that end, the cabin's entrance is situated off to the side, and recessed, to blur the lines between the indoors and the captivating greenery.

This appreciation for the natural environment also means caring for it. Considerable attention has been dedicated to the treatment of the mirror façades so as to prevent hazardous bird collisions. Bird deterrent window markers—invisible to the human eye—have been installed on the outside of the glass panes lining the living area to protect feathered wildlife, making this cabin as mindful of nature as it is pampering toward nature lovers.

FOREST GLAMP (2021), Québec, Canada

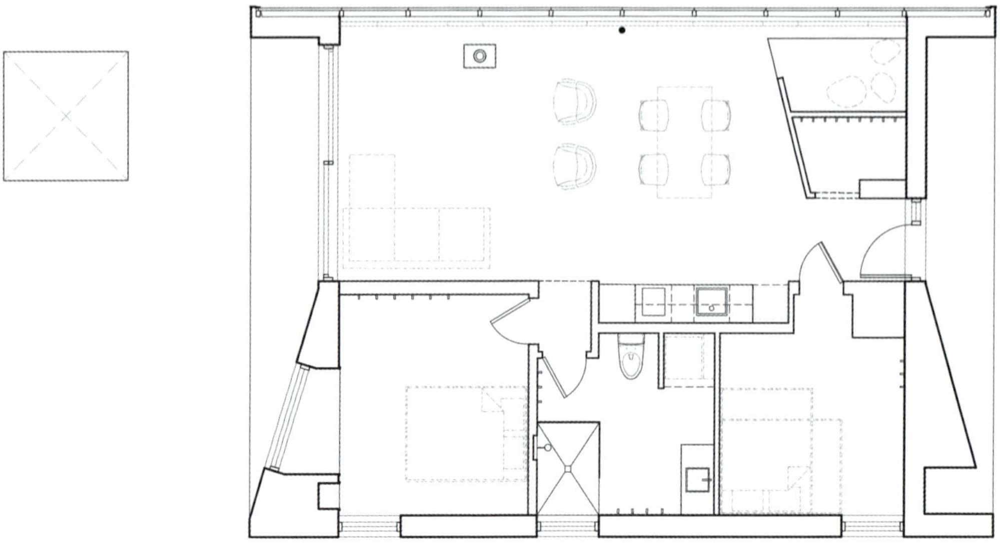

Floor plan

Simplicity for Effect

The best thing to do in this cabin is be. Here, among cacao trees and lush vegetation, in front of a small river, one lives in the moment in this refuge away from the city.

The design process behind Huaira is a construction system that is a solution without creating problems; the combination of simple processes derived from local building techniques. Plywood as a construction base combines with simple building technology—that extends a low-cost, replicable, weather adaptable, scalable, modular, removable, and expandable solution—to ensure minimal impact to the environment and maintain a negative carbon footprint.

The cabin structure is elevated to provide sufficient ventilation in the hot, humid climate and also to build a defence against heavy rains that pelt down most of the year. Doing so also generates a cold air chamber under the building. A second air chamber is created through the double-layer design of the walls and roof to further ventilate the interior space; these layers also house the structural beams. Floor and wall perforations enhance the favorable air circulation with cross ventilation flow, and the operable double layer of the roof allows control of direct sunlight without breaking the connection to the landscape.

Skylights, glass doors, and glass gables at both ends of the structure add to the range of straightforward solutions, creatively utilized in the design to draw natural light into the space and engulf the interior with reviving views of the greenery outside.

HUAIRA (2019), Puerto Quito, Ecuador

Cross section

Longitudinal section

Candle in the Woods

The gorgeous forest setting, accompanied by a picturesque lake, inspires the design of Kynttilä. Tailored to elicit the best of its surroundings, the cabin, located in eastern Finland, on the Nunnanniemi peninsula in Lake Saimaa, sits in the middle of a pristine forest looking out toward mesmerizing views over the water.

A large part of the property is set in a nature reserve and the conscientious design of the cabin results in minimum impact to the forest. The only disruption was a temporary access road that was created on the day of installation; vegetation that was removed to make way for this road was put back in place once building was completed.

The concept of Kynttilä is zen, woven around the definition of "nothing." The space aims to provide focus, visually and spiritually, by stripping the content and design intention to a bare minimum. The proportions of the structure enveloping the interior are deliberately identical, so as to frame the water view with maximized simplicity. A large window creates intimate contact with the surroundings, communicating directly with it. At night, lit from within, Kynttilä (which translates to "candle" in English) shines as a warm light on the lake shore like a candle in the woods.

Cross laminated timber (CLT) elements are used in the entire building structure, including the furniture and entrance door, and complement the exterior larch timber cladding to fashion this unique lookout toward the water, hidden amid nature's green giants.

KYNTTILÄ (2020), Lake Saimaa, Finland

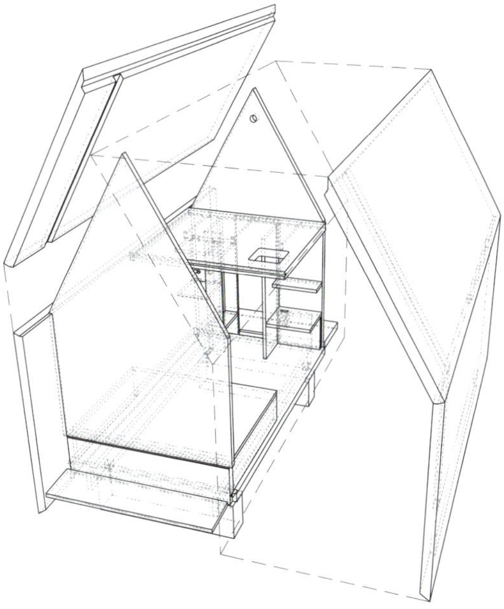

Design element diagram

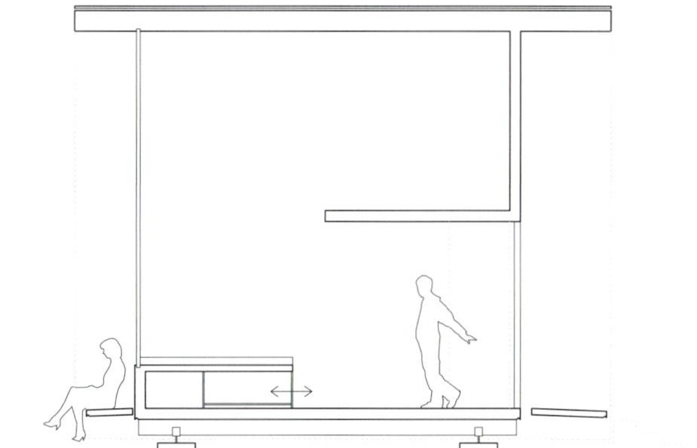

Section

Swamp Serenity

Maidla Nature Villa is a testament to great architecture on a small scale, making every inch count. Located among birch trees, at the edge of a bog, it provides a truly immersive experience in Estonia's untouched nature.

The architecture extends as much to the site—with its natural sounds, scents, and sights—as the site does to it, designed specifically to bring out the best of the location and the environment. The villa stands on 23-foot (7-meter) stilts that have been driven into the swamp soil to ensure a stable structure on the unusual ground; this also serves to preserve the birch trees around the site by minimizing disturbance to land from excavation.

The first floor and lower terrace are 3.3 feet (1 meter) above the ground to accommodate high waters during bogland flooding, which sometimes allows for an interesting experience of setting off on a canoe, right from the terrace. The night terrace offers more outdoor-enjoyment space at the height of treetops, enhancing activities like star gazing and birdwatching.

The bedroom looks out to nature through large windows, enjoying panoramic views interspersed with rich flora, birdlife, and foraging forest critters. A fireplace forms the focal point of the interior space; drapes allow flexible partitioning and use of the space.

The cabin's remote location requires minimizing the need for maintenance through durable, low-maintenance materials. Dark, thermo-treated ash covers the façade, roof, and terraces, as steel beams strengthen the rigidity of the structure.

MAIDLA NATURE VILLA (2020), Rapla County, Estonia

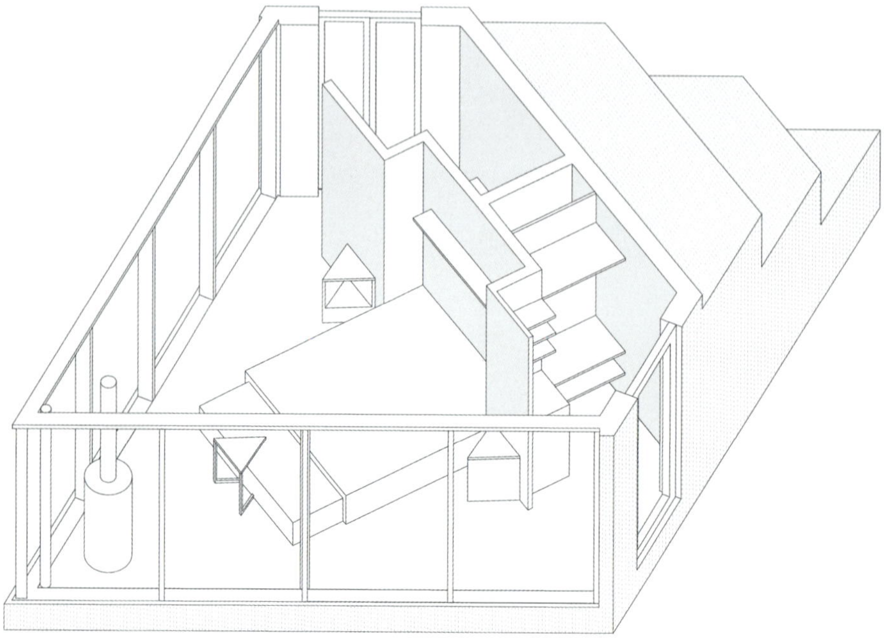

Isometric drawing

Up in the Air

Niliaitta is an ecologically sensitive accommodation that celebrates the nature on its site and the biodiversity of the land by rising above it. Set in Suomenselkä, known as "Lapland's finger," a unique region of Finland near Salamajärvi National Park, the cabin takes its name from a traditional Lapland building that stores food outdoors in habitats rampant with wildlife.

Guiding its dynamic design are aspects such as the spirit of the place, experiencing the surrounding nature, and sensory experiences like the stillness and quietness of the environment. Still in its prototype phase, Niliaitta joins two other predecessors that were inspired by the respective elements of land and water, with Niliaitta embodying the element of air.

Designed on the concept that everyday worries seem to automatically get left behind when one is lifted into the air, the cabin positions a retreat raised above the ground to encourage a removal from the stresses of fast-paced city living. This design also respects the environment, leaving untouched the many trees around the cabin and the array of animals that call them home.

Contrasting with the wild surroundings is a cozy interior that guides the experience of the cabin. A ceiling-height window extends the length of an entire wall, providing unobstructed visual connection to the surrounding nature. An intentionally neutral interior palette allows this landscape view to dominate, ensuring that the interior scenery only plays a subtle role, second to the amazing nature outside.

NILIAITTA (2020), Kivijärvi, Finland

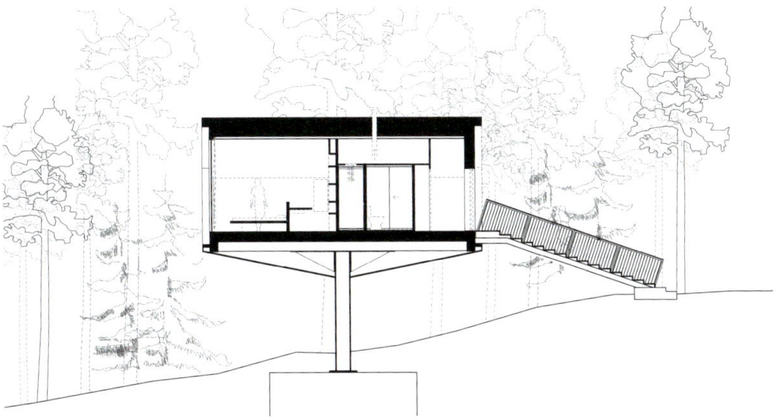

Section

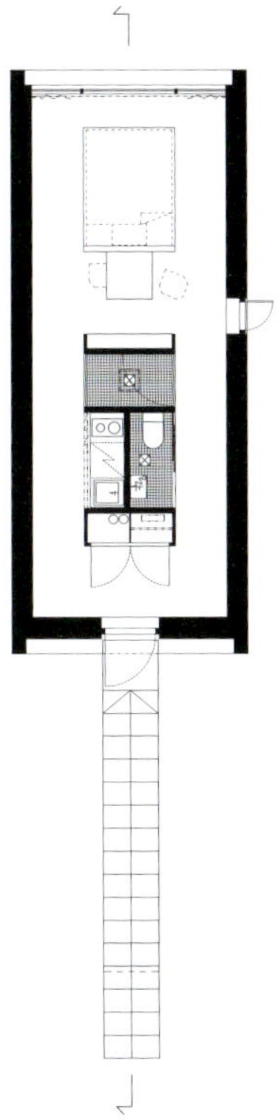

Floor plan

Country Charm

Oak Cabin is a sight for sore eyes accustomed to bustling walkways, hectic traffic, and scurrying humans, constantly in a hurry. Here, time stands still.

Contentedly nestled among lush trees and greenery by the River Teign, it paints a charming image. The cabin is crafted from oak and displays a darkened, charred cedar exterior created by the traditional Japanese *shou sugi ban* technique, which settles it discreetly into the grassy outskirts of the surrounding forest. In contrast, the interior woodwork is treated with whitening oils to evoke a lime-washed, Scandinavian feel. This light, airy interior is enhanced by floor-to-ceiling windows that frame picturesque views of the valley, while letting in lots of natural light. It is also fitted with ample concealed storage that utilizes every inch of space to maximize the layout; aesthetic amplifications are taken care of by a solid ash and oak kitchen with custom brass handles, and a sleek Carrara marble shower.

Self-contained and solar powered, Oak Cabin is fully equipped to support a comfortable off-grid lifestyle. Water is drawn from a nearby well; a wood burner at the heart of the space provides heat; and south-facing windows help pull in the sun's warmth during winter. An oak deck under a cooling awning at the front of the cabin also offers a secluded shaded spot for relaxing among the wild surroundings, or delving into a book as leaves rustle in the background.

OAK CABIN (2017), Devon, United Kingdom

Coming Home

The possibilities offered by this modular cabin are endless, with a system that allows it the freedom to be anything—an extra bedroom; a gym; or a home office, in just about any location. Originally designed as a response to the ongoing pandemic, it redefines the notion of a "home away from home" to negotiate restrictions that limited the range of travel. No matter where it is placed—be it a backyard, rooftop terrace, or even the nearby forest—the cabin is a spatial solution that allows one to find one's own space and peace of mind, without leaving "home."

An integral aspect of the design is its versatility and adaptability. The outer wooden structure acts as a blank slate, while the interior is adjustable to individual preferences; custom furniture attaches to the wooden structure on rungs, giving the freedom to tailor the space as desired.

The guiding emphasis of the design seeks to express that a minimal space, with only the essentials, can be enjoyable and restorative. In line with this, the structure is not insulated, connecting natural elements and ever-changing weather conditions outside as closely as possible to the inhabitant. Ecologically sourced Finnish wood allows the cabin to withstand harsh arctic winters, while remaining cozy and nest-like inside through warm wooden tones and colors. To enable access to hard-to-reach remote locations, the cabin is strategically light enough for transportation by crane or helicopter. A resilient foundation supports all types of sites, also adding to its versatility.

SPACE OF MIND (2020), Porvoo, Finland

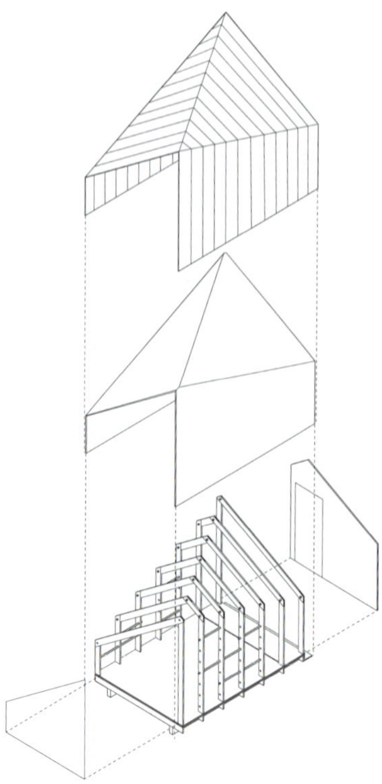

Axonometric drawing

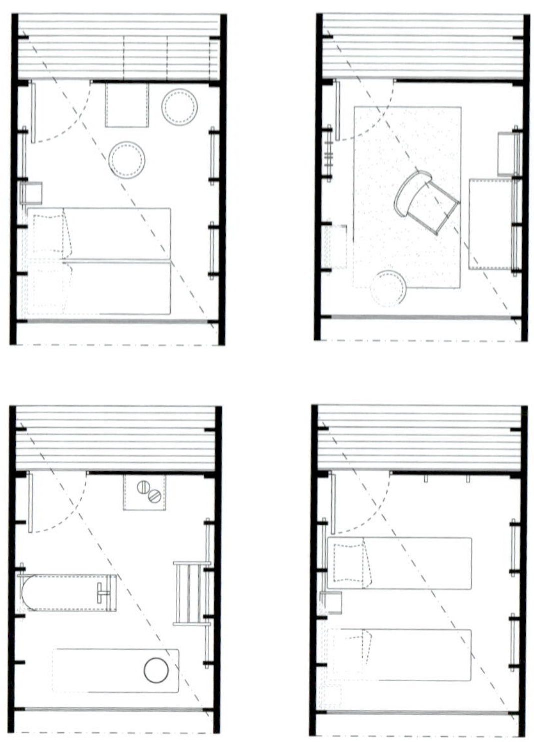

Floor plans: alternative layouts

Nature's Nest

Literally nestled in tall pine trees, this cabin, located in the forested hillside around the Hardanger fjord near Odda, Norway, makes every day exhilarating. In creating a unique experience that connects to the physical and emotional sensation of climbing and exploring a tree, the cabin tailors an opportunity to pause and appreciate the natural environment and the rhythm of the forest.

The experience begins with a walk along the edge of the fjord and up through the forest on a steep, winding path. At the site, a small timber bridge finally makes real the childhood fantasy, as it leads off the ground, up into the living pine tree, and into the cabin suspended 16.4 to 19.7 feet (5 to 6 meters) above the forest floor. Organized around the central tree trunk are four sleep/rest zones, a bathroom, a kitchen, and a living space that leaves little to desire with a spellbinding view; it sweeps generously across a magnificent scenery of green pine trees, down to the glassy waters of the fjord below, and on to the mountains in the periphery and beyond.

In its appreciation of timber as a building material, the cabin experiments with the material potential of wood, in part inspired by the Norwegian cultural traditions of vernacular timber architecture. The cabin is formed from a series of radial glue-laminated (glulam) timber ribs; the untreated timber shingles encase the volume in a protective skin, which will weather over time to blend the cabin with the natural patina of the forest.

WOODNEST (2020), Odda, Norway

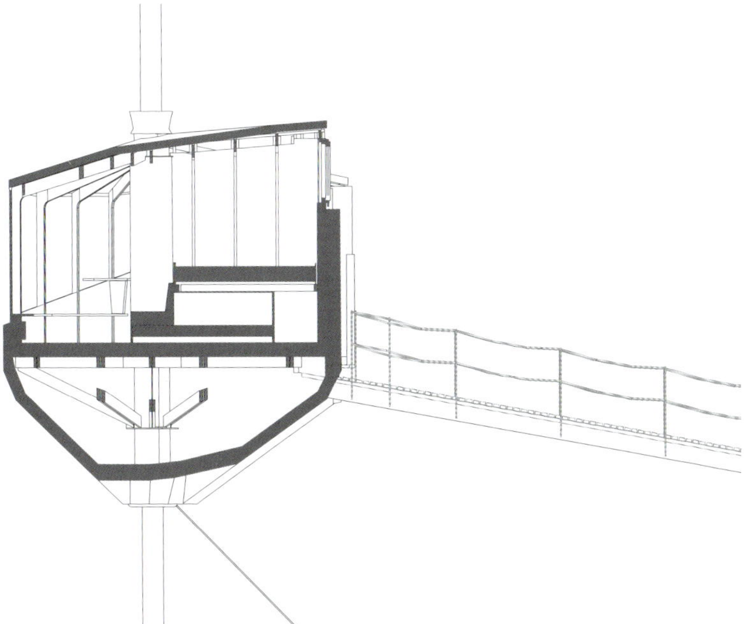

Section

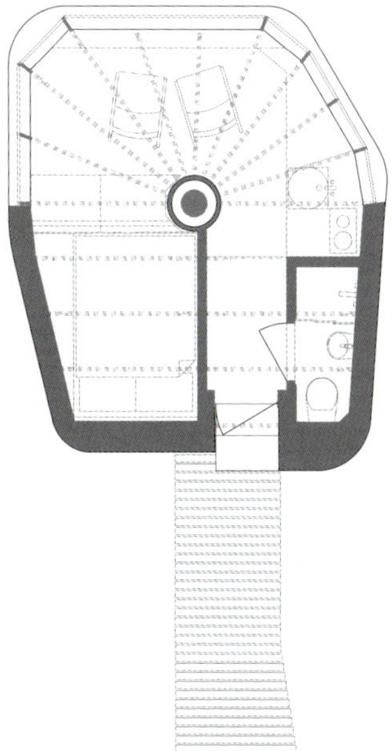

Floor plan

Mountain Perches

Facing the grandeur of mighty mountains, one comes to understand the meaning of true freedom. Overlooking misty valleys and ice caps, these high-altitude havens keep adventurers safe and warm, offering the best seat in the house to watch the show.

The Edge of Transcendence

Blue-hued valleys and misty gray peaks that pierce the clouds form the accompanying scenery for this cabin located on the Marmarole mountain range in Italy, 8,750 feet (2,667 meters) above sea level. The challenges that faced this high-altitude architecture were composed of rock, light, wind, snow, and distance. The design also needed to address the following: the desire to explore and move in the perception of the expanded space created by the high altitude; the need to protect oneself and take refuge; and the need to rediscover a human dimension.

Finding its dimension in the possibility of perceptive amplification, the cabin attempts to circumscribe the surroundings to define a break that seeks out a temporary border to the landscape that looks upon a progressive compression of rocks, light, wind, and snow. Through a rough-hewn volume placed so adventurously that it seems almost as if it is teetering on the edge, the cabin frames the breathtaking landscape and connects person and environment.

The interior is iterated in a wooden belly that softens the impact of the rigid landscape. It opens a spatial dimension beyond its own internal geometry, anchored by an inclining profile that aligns the internal space upward, arranging it along the longitudinal axis. Defined by nature, Bivouac Fanton allows one to be transported—disappearing into the snow, to be swept up by the wind, lifted by the greatness of an absolute landscape.

BIVOUAC FANTON (2021), Dolomites (Belluno), Italy

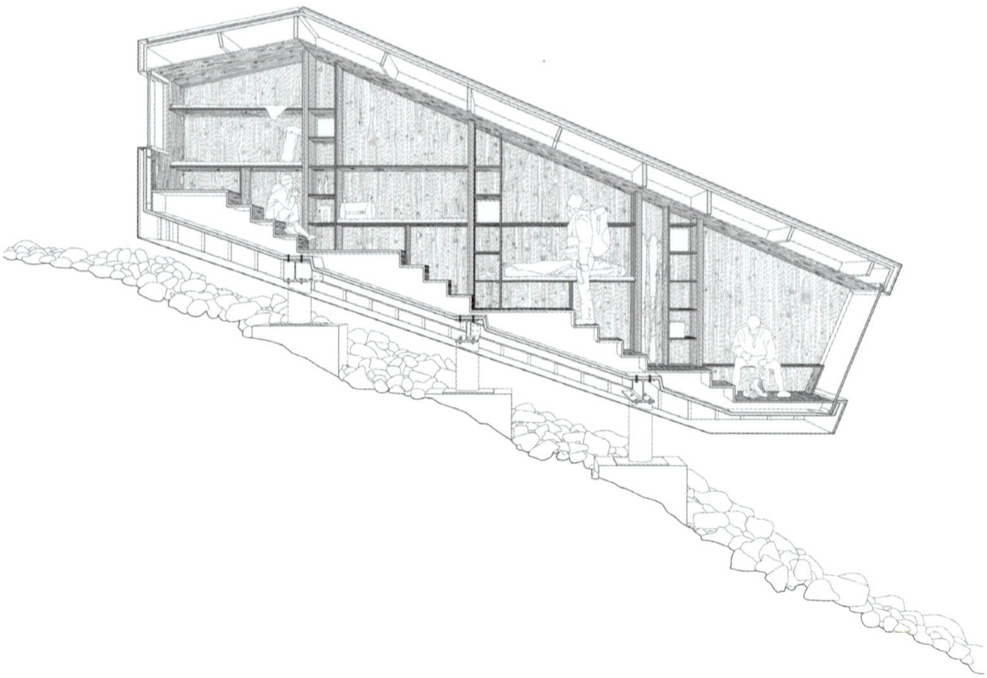

Section

A Sensitive Solution

What if you could build a cabin in the mountain range of Suntikoopa, Coorg, India, just the way you like it, in just two weeks?

Cabin A24 is the first in a series of prefabricated units that are manufactured off-site and designed to be assembled on-site within fourteen days. Though small, measuring only 225 square feet (20.9 square meters), the cabin includes all amenities that one needs to live off-grid, as comfortably as possible.

Originally inspired by the search for a sustainable and sensitive solution to living among nature, which would respect the natural biodiversity of the land, Cabin A24 is the result of collaborations between the owners and developers, with the architects finally bringing the concept home. Nestled within a coffee estate, the cabin is designed to express the zeitgeist of the current times through its contemporary take on a forest cabin, while allowing its natural context to take center stage in curating the spatial experience.

Every corner in the cabin strives to visually, if not spatially, connect with the surroundings, be it the bathroom—which comes furnished with all the modern amenities—the kitchenette, or the living space, which captures stunning views of the valley through the large, open façade. A sleek, contemporary form expresses a strong architectural identity that is complemented with refined interiors. The cabin is conceptualized as a system of fixed and flexible elements, with furniture, lighting, fixtures, and bathroom and material finishes customized to preference.

CABIN A24 (2021), Coorg, India

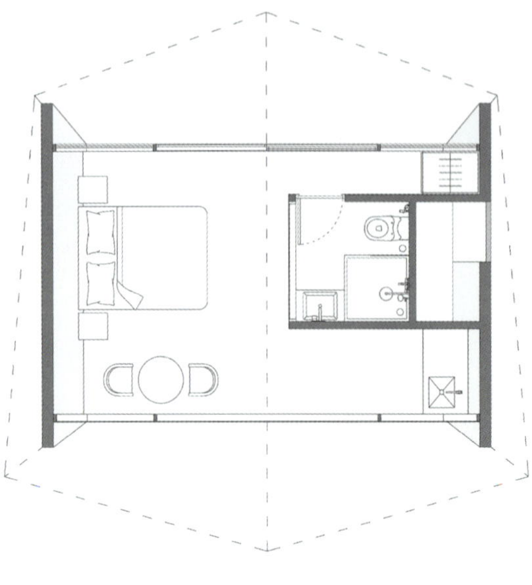

Floor plan

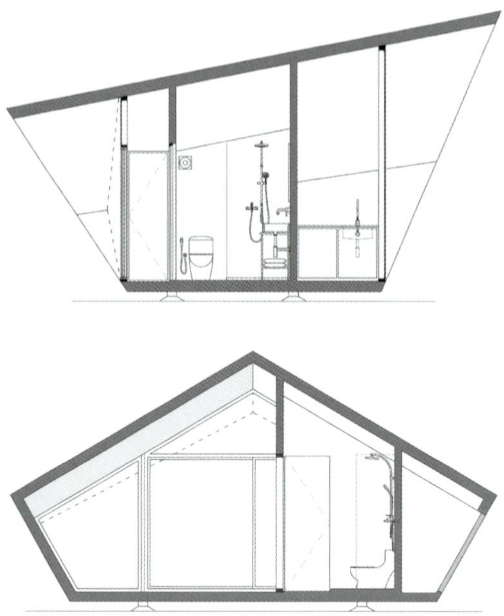

Sections

Arctic Outlook

Set above the Arctic Circle, these hiking cabins overlook breathtaking scenery: glorious sunrises that ascend from the horizon and luminous dances of the Northern Lights that paint the night sky. Conceived as organic wooden structures, the cabins fit harmoniously with the local terrain and provide hikers with a warm, inviting rest stop that withstands harsh polar winters.

Collaborating with FORMAT Engineers, SPINN Arkitekter brings the concept sketch into reality, transforming a double-curved wooden structure that can be precisely manufactured to be built on top of a mountain, and assembled by volunteers. The site was mapped in 3D using a drone and photogrammetry software to give a detailed map of the surface, which was used as a baseline for form-finding. The initial shapes made by the architects in Sketchup and Rhino were further optimized and transformed by the engineers using Kangaroo and Grasshopper, together with some customized scripting tools developed by FORMAT. The result: a wooden, cross-laminated timber shell with seventy-seven unique panels that fit together like a 3D puzzle.

The design was also tested against simulated wind conditions to make sure that it would withstand winter arctic storms and extreme wind conditions. Snow simulations also ensured that the entrance remains snow-free, as intended. The first cabin was assembled in approximately 1,500 hours by volunteers; the only professional work on the project was the two-layer bitumen waterproofing of the shell and the pouring of the foundation on-site. The cabin was then lifted into place and winched together, with the window, fireplace, ramp, and interior furniture fitted into place on-site.

HAMMERFEST HIKING CABINS (2019), Hammerfest, Norway

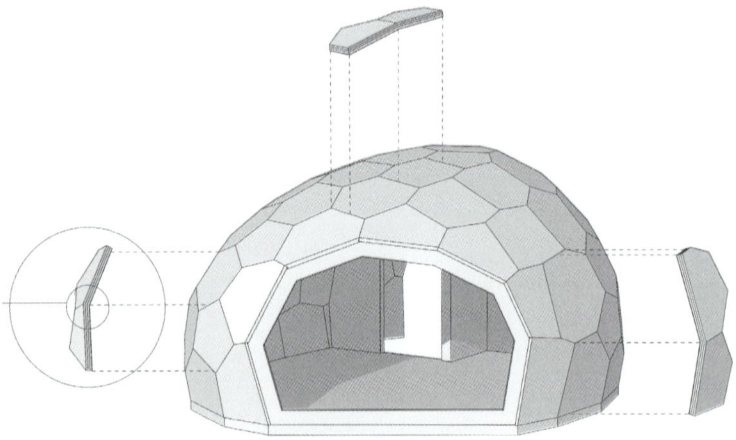

Cabin construction diagram

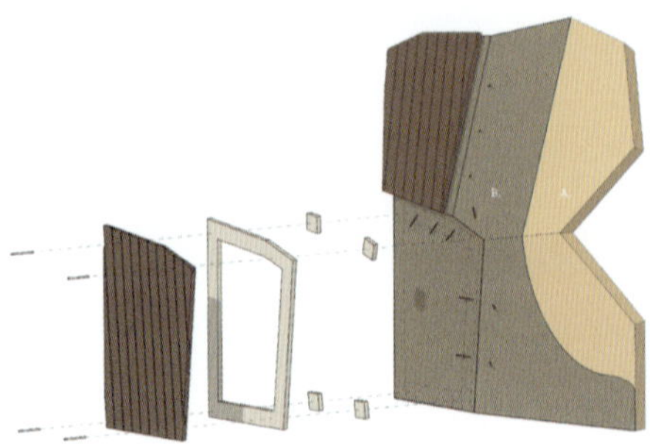

Cladding panel assembly diagram

Refuge for Reflection

Set among snow-capped Chilean mountain peaks, this mountain hiking cabin allows for a night of rest before continuing on the journey.

The concept design results in a cabin that is built through planes and angles, with a structure that provides an entrance through its folds, and exterior views through its cuts. Built around a central core of services, the exterior shape and interior volume are defined by the folds.

At one end of the cabin is the bedroom, along with a storage room for mountaineering equipment. The other end features a sitting area where the nearby mountain draws the eye toward the panoramic view. The exterior is finished in pine, metal elements, and picture windows that perform both structural and volumetric functions.

The cabin rests on piles, to be a self-contained object suspended above the ground. The building is ventilated on all sides; the updraft from the mountain provides airflow through a series of dedicated openings. As a point of arrival and departure for mountaineers on their treks, the cabin is more than a mere lookout or shelter, but also is a unique place for contemplation and reflection set amid the peaceful silence of the mountains. It is truly a refuge among nature's towering guardians.

MOUNTAINEER'S REFUGE (2016), Valparaíso región, Chile

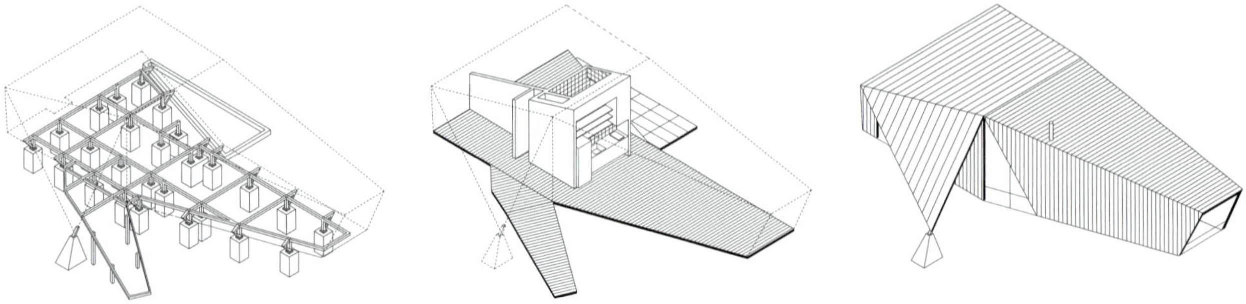

Axonometric construction drawings

Cabins in the Clouds

The Tungestølen cluster of cabins is situated on a small plateau that overlooks the stunning Jostedalen glacier in Luster, western Norway. These cabins replace the original Tungestølen Tourist Cabin destroyed by cyclone Dagmar in December 2011. The new cabins offer a comfortable and generous shelter in structures meticulously designed to withstand the fast-changing weather conditions of the mountainous site.

To navigate the wrath of future extreme climate, a constellation of nine robust pentagonal and oblique cabins were designed, made with wooden glulam frames, covered by sheets of CLT, and clad in pine. The outward-facing walls have a beak-like shape to slow down strong winds sweeping up from the valley floor. Inside, the playful shape of the cabins frames the mountains and valleys through angular and panoramic windows that introduce captivating views and natural light.

The main cabin houses a space well suited for collective meals around generous wooden tables. A high ceiling creates a spacious social point with panoramic views overlooking the surrounding landscape, complemented by a comfortable lounge and a large stone-clad fireplace. The remaining cabins consist of a dormitory and a smaller private unit offering approximately thirty visitors a comfortable refuge for the night. The steep mountains on all sides afford unparalleled views and a dramatic landscape that makes the cabins an ideal starting point for adept hikers, as well as families with small children taking less advanced hikes.

TUNGESTØLEN HIKING CABINS (2019), Luster, Norway

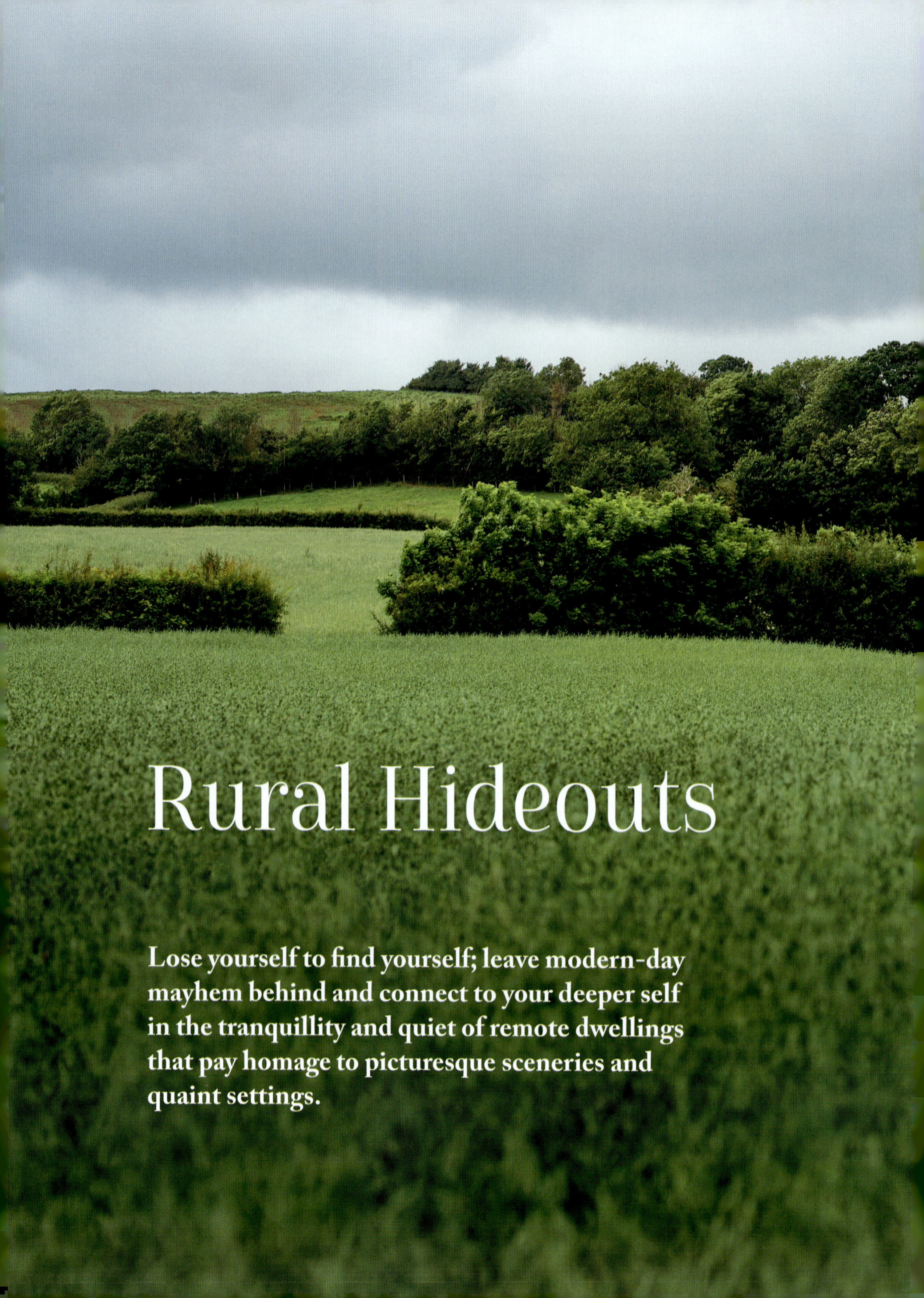

Rural Hideouts

Lose yourself to find yourself; leave modern-day mayhem behind and connect to your deeper self in the tranquillity and quiet of remote dwellings that pay homage to picturesque sceneries and quaint settings.

Island Ideals

This island retreat is a highly crafted minimalist residence inspired by traditional Japanese houses. Designed to present like a piece of furniture, with most furnishings built-in, the cabin makes room for only the essentials: enjoying the simple pleasures: star-gazing, and connecting with nature. The only pieces of furniture in this unique refuge are a low table and mattress in the sleeping loft.

As the site is off-grid, the cabin collects its own rainwater. It is also powered by photovoltaics and heated by a woodfire oven; gas provides hot water and stovetop cooking. The views to the north are overshadowed by a tall dense forest, while the views to the south are expansive. Thus, the cabin opens onto an east- and west-facing deck to catch the morning and afternoon sun and still afford glimpses of alluring scenery. Translucent glass sliding doors that reference the luminosity of Japanese paper screens create a sense of enclosure and privacy at night; they also prevent birds, including the endangered swift parrot, from flying into the building and striking the glass.

A high roof allows solar panels and a skylight to catch sun from over the trees to the north, while a light-colored interior timber décor imparts coziness and a sense of "otherness" and escape. An entrance pergola creates storage and, together with underground water tanks, allows the cabin to function independently. The Nectre Bakers Oven provides ample heating for the cabin using fallen timber around the site, with the romance of a flame fire and hearty meals in winter.

BRUNY ISLAND HIDEAWAY (2017), Bruny Island, Tasmania, Australia

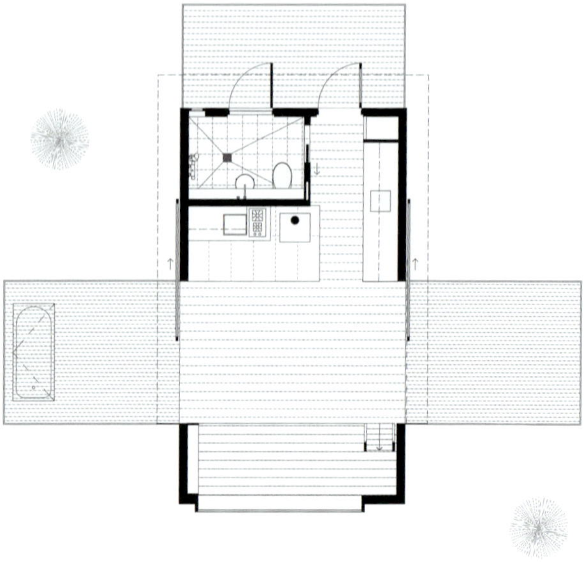

First-floor plan

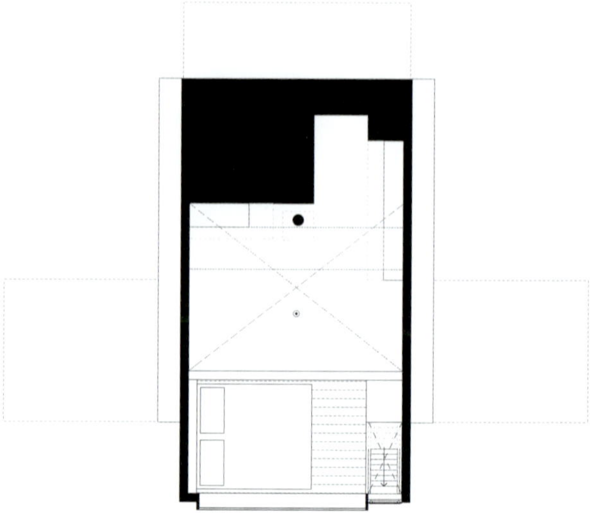

Second-floor plan

Convenient Cabana

A timeless experience in nature, away from the chaos of modern-day life, is what the compact Cabana lays claim to. A flexible, sustainable building system, accommodated to any space and location, with little interference to the environment, together with a functional, natural timber interior, ensure the cabin makes good on this claim.

To reduce environmental impact, steel, cement slab, and reforestation wood form the structure and sealing materials, in the process minimizing material waste through leftovers, water consumption, and CO_2 emissions. Rock wool in the walls and ceiling, as well as large PVC frames (known for their excellent sealing capability) aid in thermal, lighting, and acoustic comfort. The frames secure openings that are strategically positioned to facilitate cross ventilation, and work in tandem with LED strip lighting and a wood burning stove. These implements strive toward reducing the need for air conditioning and maximizing the performance of artificial lighting, in order to reduce electricity consumption.

Environmental impact is also lessened through a metallic pile foundation, using only the amount of concrete necessary for the pile shoes. The cabin can be sited in most terrains, but if necessary, a new foundation can be customized, specific to the terrain.

The cabin can be built in remote locations through a modular assembly system that can be easily carried by two people. There is no need for cranes, allowing the cabin to be transported in a one-box truck (reducing logistics costs) and set-up quickly in the most hard-to-access locations within the day.

CABANA (2021), Belo Horizonte, Brazil

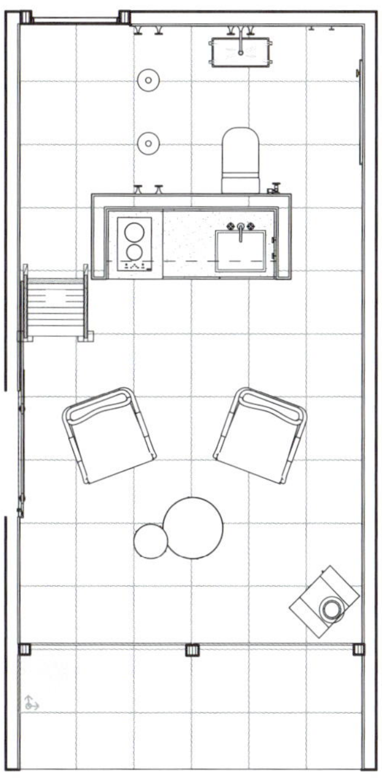

First-floor plan

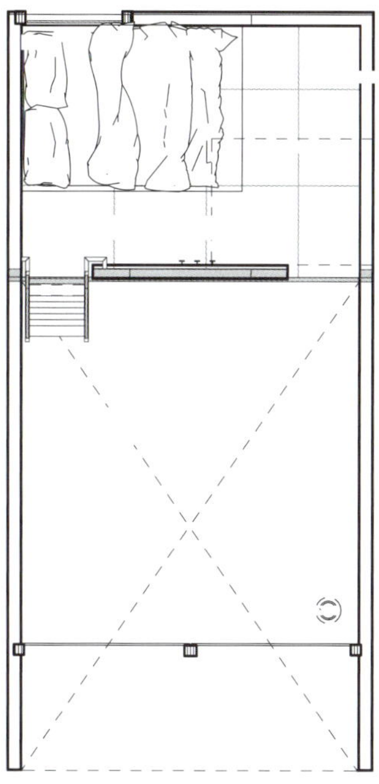

Mezzanine floor plan

Fun and Games

Taking design and aesthetic cues from its predecessor, the WorkStation cabin, the revamped GameStation cabin is tailored for gamers to enjoy an exclusive, specially crafted nook to slay dragons and build empires.

The same eye-catching polygonal shape of the WorkStation cabin is rendered in the GameStation unit, but with a mattress flooring instead of wood. When sitting on the floor, the protruding walls of the polygon become comfortable backrests to lean on through long hours of playing video games or watching movies, cozily wrapped up.

The cabin also presents an innovative quality space that is suited as a comfortable accommodation despite its small size, thanks to its highly functional, well-thought-out fittings and fixtures.

Walls are sound- and heat-insulated, so that the space can also be used as an extra room or even as a stand-alone tiny house. A clever, ready-to-assemble structure allows the cabin to be set up quickly and easily, either at the end of the garden, on an empty plot, on the waterfront, or in the yard of an office building (or even inside it).

This cabin makes room to inspire owners to implement their own ideas within it, to make it truly one of a kind.

GAMESTATION CABIN (2021), Budapest, Hungary

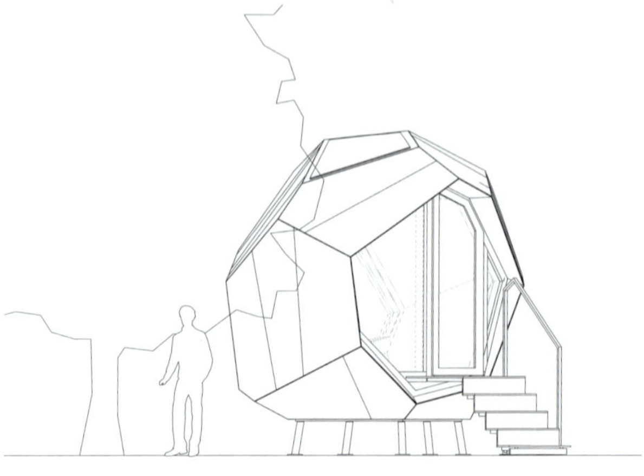

Elevation

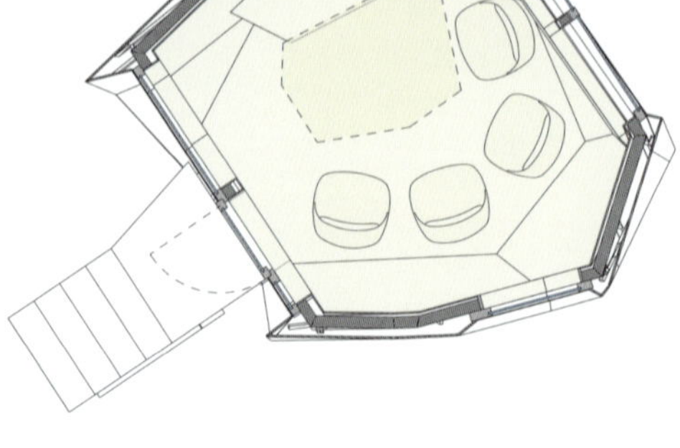

Floor plan

Rich History

Named after the historical owner of the property, Benjamin Gawthorne, Gawthorne's Hut is an experience that responds directly to the history and context of its property through repurposed materials and design references. The angled galvanized shell and rich timber interior reference the predominant rural vernacular of hay sheds and outbuildings, in particular an existing hay shed that was destroyed by a storm in 2017. The angled roof, while referencing the remnants of the shed, also accommodates the solar array on the building. Internally, the inclined form is emphasized through a blackbutt-lined ceiling, which also frames the valley views to the east.

Repurposed bricks from Gawthorne's original chimney and fireplace form a low-height brick wall in the interior that separates bathroom functions in an otherwise open plan—designed such to maximize the cabin's small footprint. Minimal joinery extends this openness, while the wall doubles as a cover for services that come down from the ceiling.

The concealment of the services is well thought out, so as not to detract from the picturesque rural setting and cabin experience. A large galvanized metal clad door to the western façade conceals services out of sight, opening to reveal storage, solar batteries, an inverter, an electrical board, and a gas hot-water unit. The location of services here also provides a heavy buffer to the western sun. The cabin achieves a BAL 12.5 bushfire rating, and incorporates sustainable design elements like rain water storage, thermal mass regulation, and passive solar shading, among others.

GAWTHORNE'S HUT (2020), Mudgee, New South Wales, Australia

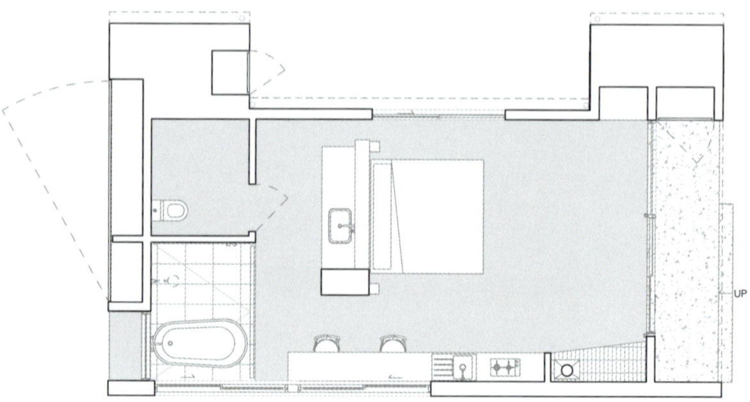

Floor plan

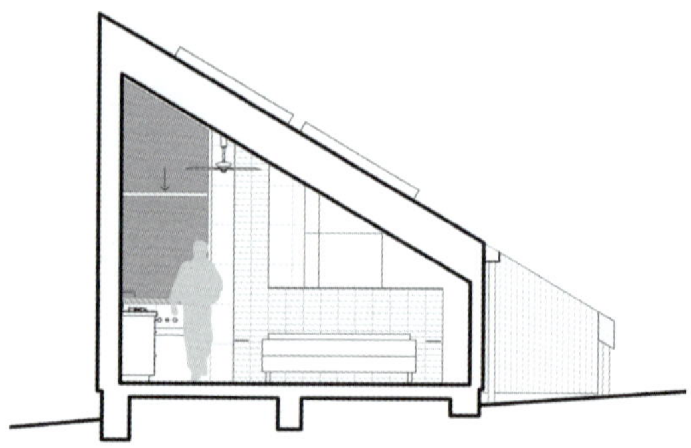

Section

nectre

Rural Paradise

Holly Water Cabin seeks to invite its inhabitants into a close relationship with the outdoors, all the while embracing them in the utmost comfort. Designed to extend rural farm stays to guests, the cabin is approached via a picturesque path that winds through a corn field.

Clad in cedar sourced from a local mill in Dartmoor, United Kingdom, the cabin's exterior is characterized by a large mono-pitch roof with generous eaves. The building is constructed around a Douglas fir frame, and is raised off the ground on pier foundations to minimize the need for concrete. Plant-based insulation extends a high degree of insulation, as a high specification of membrane and envelope details for longevity and energy efficiency.

The interior is anchored by an oak kitchen that occupies the back wall of the open-plan interior; a bathroom and cozy sleeping area that accommodates a double bed are tucked into the gable elevation. Sliding doors open the living space onto a sweeping larch veranda with a copper tub, to create a special "among nature" experience during bath times. Interior walls are covered in a clay render as a natural alternative to plaster; the clay finish also connects the inside of the cabin to the nature outside, and helps maintain a breathable building envelope to regulate humidity and temperature, and provides a natural organic texture that is pleasing to the eye. A calm color palette using other natural materials throughout also harmonizes the cabin with the surrounding landscape.

HOLLY WATER CABIN (2020), Devon, United Kingdom

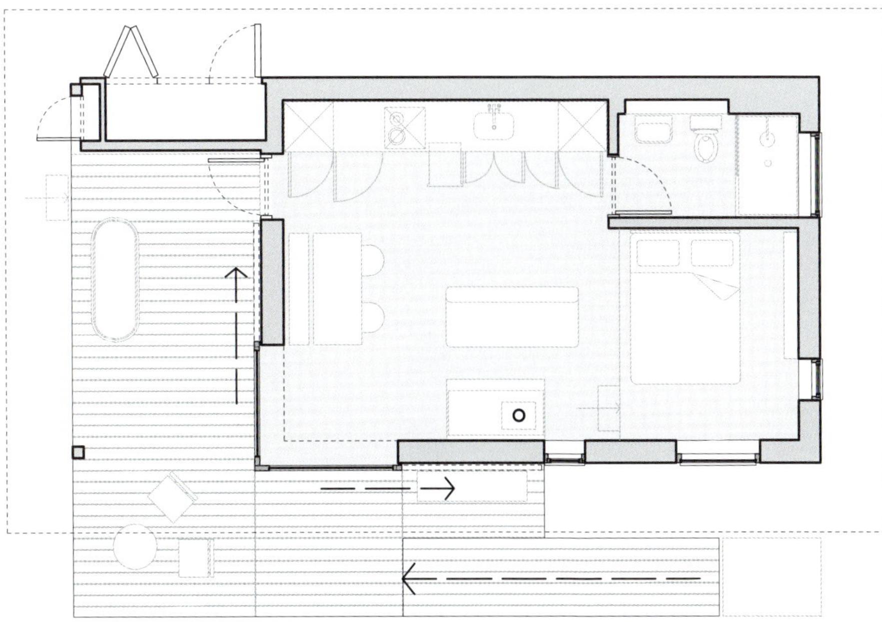

Floor plan

Strong Connections

Through an optimal interplay between design, construction, and use of materials, this prefabricated cabin allows design freedom, a quick building process, and minimal environmental impact. A modular building system uses prefabricated elements of flexible dimensions that are assembled on-site, allowing a free layout decided by the occupant; numerous options are available for finishing the roof, façade, and interior. This allows inhabitants to have a hand in building their home, while enabling the cabin to be customized, built DIY, and respond to site and environmental conditions.

The featured project has been built for clients who sketched the design along with the architects. A clever spatial layout separates the living area and sleeping area with a spacious hall that accommodates gatherings and social activities. This zoning also yields smart, separated climatic zones.

Prefab concrete beams and pier blocks make up the foundation that is placed on the underlying sandy soil, so that the cabin leaves no trace when removed. The floor below is insulated around the edges only, so that the thermal mass of the ground under the house is utilized, providing extra cooling in the summer, while flattening out the heat curve in the winter—courtesy of the buffering capacity of the sand. The cabin runs on electricity generated from a collective project nearby, as the extensive shade of the trees challenges solar power accumulation. The underfloor heating, which can also cool, is powered by an air-to-water heat pump. The cabin can be transported by road within the European Union (EU); depending on suitable construction partners, projects outside the EU are also possible.

INDIGO CABIN (2019), Barchem, The Netherlands

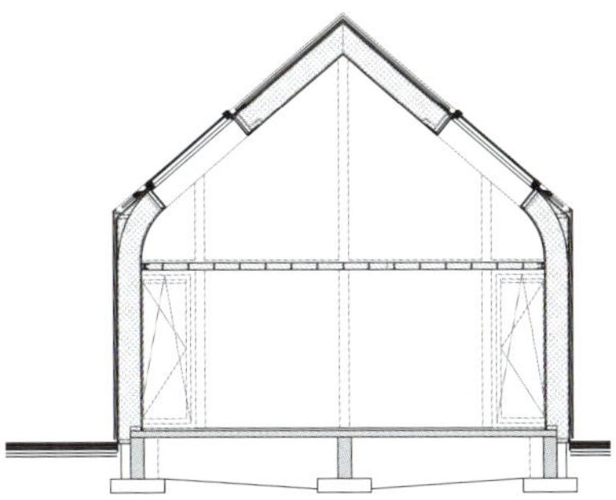

Cross section

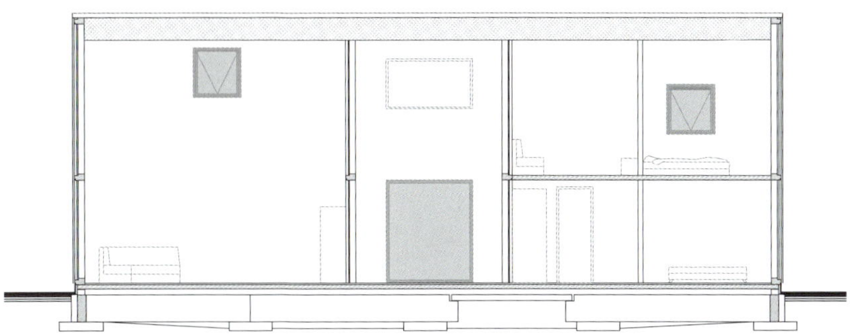

Long section

Making the Most

Taking key points from Scandinavian design aesthetics, this cabin propounds the Nordic concept of *friluftsliv* (pronounced *free*-loofts-liv), which translates to "open-air living"—described by Norwegian poet Henrik Ibsen as "the value of spending time in the remote outdoors for spiritual and mental wellbeing." It is an "off-the-shelf" housing solution that extends the opportunity to immerse in nature, while arranging its modular elements to suit the need of the inhabitant and the site.

Each living space is conceptualized as a separate design exercise, allowing various configurations that can be added to, or taken from, to organize a variety of living and sleeping spaces, and even a sauna and outdoor shower. Expansive, concealed storage walls maximize floor space and maintain a clean aesthetic in the small footprint, as cozy nooks and generous bespoke window seats create memorable user experiences and connect the inhabitant to the outdoors. Each bedroom extends a private retreat within the landscape, enhanced by key pieces of furniture (such as fold-down beds) and a décor specially curated to create a calm environment.

A large glazed façade floods the interior of the cabin with natural light and looks out to the inviting natural surroundings, but can also be orientated to ensure privacy. A "fabric-first" approach to energy efficiency ensures long-term, low-energy performance with an emphasis on low-toxicity, natural, and sustainable materials. Designed to last a lifetime, the cabin is predominantly wood based, and therefore able to sequester carbon within the fabric of the building, such that it delivers a carbon negative construction.

KOTO MUUTAMA CABIN (2018), Belfast, Northern Ireland

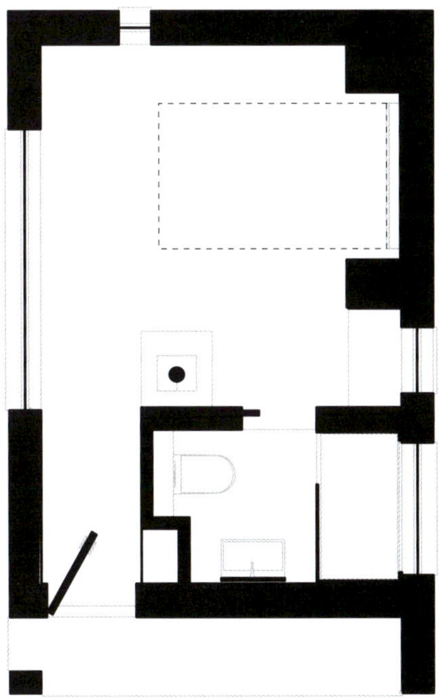

Floor plan

Surrounded by Nature

With this tiny cabin, you can disconnect from modern living and lose yourself in nature's beauty, armed with a glass of wine, ready to yield to absolute relaxation. Part of the tini® tinyhome series, tini® XS, with an area of 129 square feet (12 square meters), is a prefabricated module that is assembled in Spain, in just sixty days, to be transported to any location in the world.

Fully furnished and customizable, it can be set on any type of site to take its inhabitant all the way out into nature. The expressive Corten steel façade and structure feature a rugged finish that blends with the landscape, without intruding upon it or taking away from its natural allure. This exterior roughness is contrasted with a cozy, cocooning interior, composed of ceiling and walls wrapped with poplar OSB, and a natural oak floor that imparts soothing neutral tones to create an intimate ambiance. Elegant, moss-green window frames play off this neutral interior to add a touches of delicate embellishment that are aesthetically complementing, as they are functional, tailoring the envelope to further integrate it among natural greenery in the surroundings.

An insulation of recycled cotton, plus a continuous reflective thermal insulation layer, ensures a temperature-regulated interior. tini® XS is an outdoor home, office, or studio, adapted to suit varied uses with only one aim: pack away the stresses of modern life and connect to the beauty and solace of nature.

TINI XS (2022), Plasencia, Spain

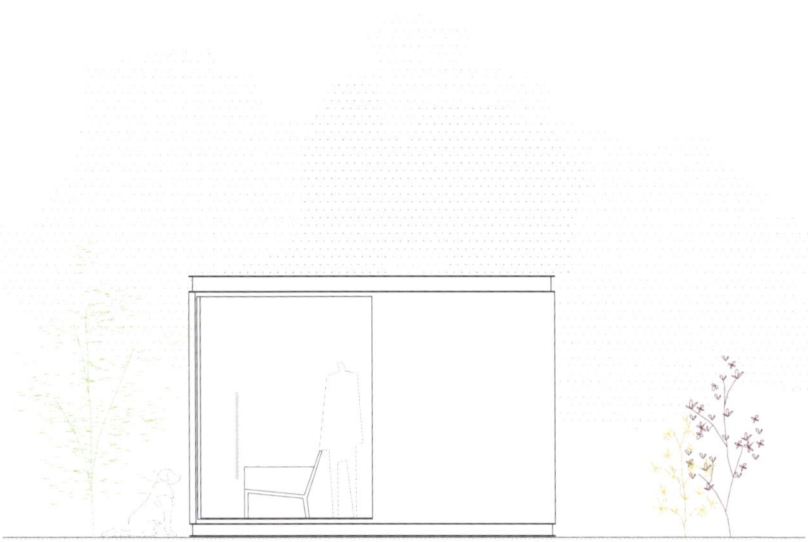

Elevation

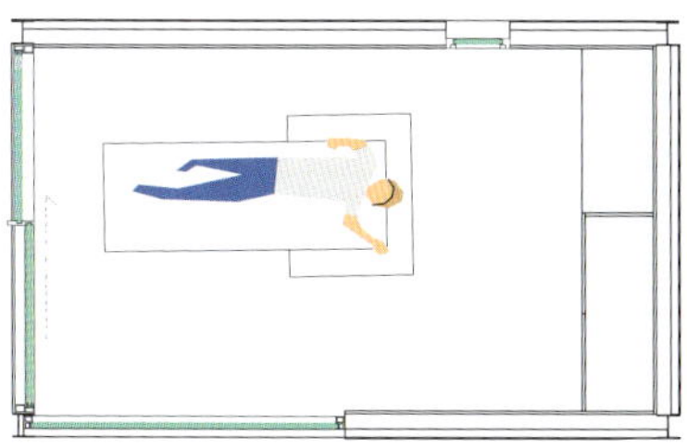

Floor plan

A Moving Experience

Inspired by trailer homes, this TOW (tiny on wheels) accommodation rethinks one's typical way of living with a dwelling that is mobile and aesthetically engaging. Developed together with the owners, the Ursa cabin arranges two sleeping areas for two people, a workstation, kitchen, full bathroom, and an outdoor deck.

The structure is composed of a primary steel frame and a secondary wooden frame. The interior walls and ceiling are covered with birch plywood panels, with the exterior covered in heat-treated timber, also known as thermowood (thermally modified wood). A thermal envelope and 1.56-inch-thick (40-millimeter-thick) expanded cork boards create insulation, as solid plywood and double glazing with tempered glass fashion doors and windows.

The exterior thermowood slats give the cabin an eye-catching appearance, looking almost shack-like. They also provide privacy and shading against the hot Portuguese sun. Heated to high temperatures in a controlled, no-oxygen environment—thus altering the chemical structures of the wood's cell walls—the thermowood slats offer a sustainable wood alternative with increased durability against the elements.

A three-stage reverse osmosis filter installed under the sink provides drinking water; used water is stored in a tank and reused for watering the plants. The water pump, water heater, refrigerator, and glass-ceramic cooktop are all powered by five solar panels on the roof, installed facing south, and can be adjusted up to a 30 percent inclination to maximize energy production in all seasons of the year; a dry toilet uses electricity to compost waste, allowing total off-grid living.

URSA TOW (2020), Cascais, Portugal

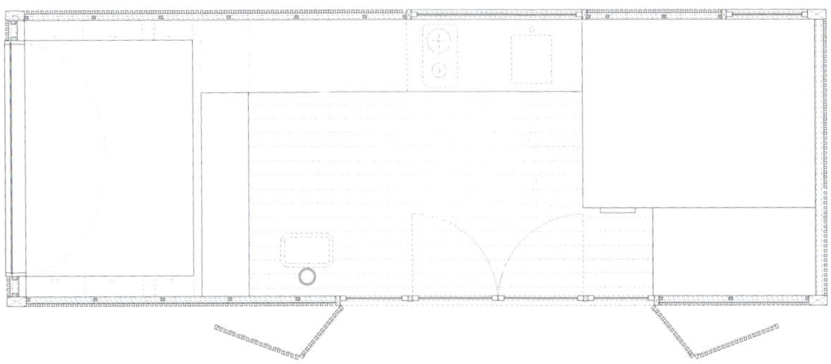

Mezzanine floor plan

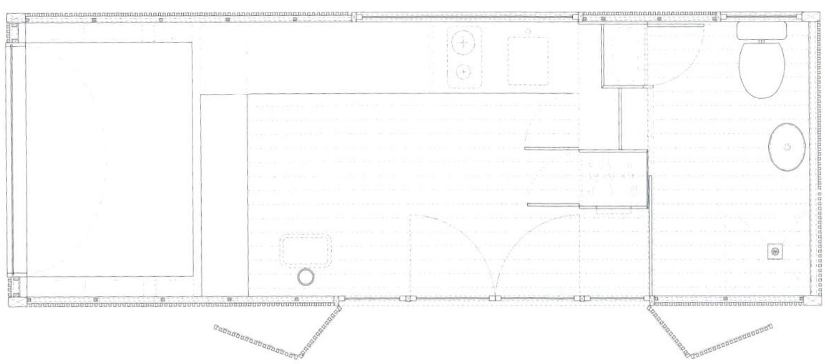

First-floor plan

Utopian Vision

Resting firmly on its high steel columns overlooking the Sabinal River, Utopia Cabin is a place of refuge. Intentionally isolated from civilization, the private cabin retreat invites inhabitants to engage with the natural surroundings. Avid naturalists, the owners wanted a place of thoughtful repose away from hectic urban life.

On arrival to the property, one navigates a gravel road to the barn, which serves as the power station with a 10-kW photovoltaic array with battery storage. Automobiles remain at the barn while guests follow a soft gravel mulched path eliciting a gentle crunching sound as they cross into the oak-forested landscape, leaving the technological world behind. At the end of the path, guests embark on a long steel ramp ascending into the tree canopies at the level of the birds.

Positioned parallel to the river, the cabin is built on the lowest bank. It is elevated lightly above the ground on steel columns, imparting minimal disturbance to the site while offering framed vistas of the surrounding riverine landscape. An expansive covered deck allows views over the landscape to the river beyond, while the interior provides views into the forested landscape. The structure's subtle modernity combined with the stimulative impact of place enhances an overall sense of quietness and reverence for its natural surroundings.

UTOPIA CABIN (2017), Utopia, Texas, United States

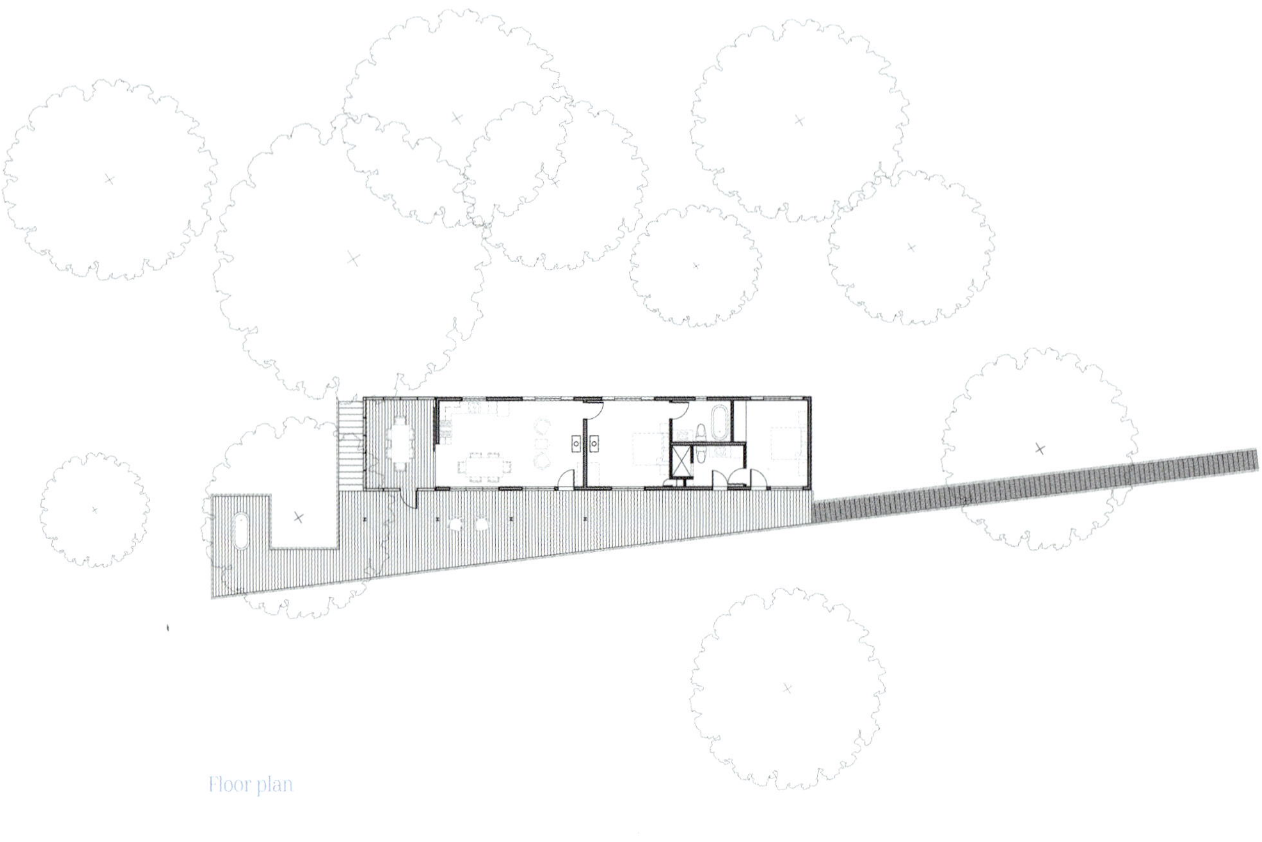

Floor plan

Tejano
OLD PLACES NEW SPACES

Natural Expressions

This cabin, located in Mae Rim district in Chiang Mai, Thailand, looks out to a gorgeous mountain view. Its imposing wooden structure houses an upper bedroom, bathrooms, a living room, pantry, and a terrace. The exterior of the building is clad on three sides with a wooden wall to create privacy, while the back opens to the landscape and a peaceful scenery of trees and vegetation.

The cabin is built using mostly local materials, using repurposed wood collected from all over Chiang Mai. The main source of pride lies in the exterior cladding, built by hand, by local carpenters. Using the Japanese *shou sugi ban* technique, the repurposed planks are sorted, sanded, and burnt on the surface to extend their lifespan. In the process, the wood is given a new life and lends the exterior a unique weathered appeal. This locally sourced Thai wood is also more resistant to weather conditions than other types of imported wood.

With this cabin, the architects aim to show the beautiful creation that is possible through expressive design and local materials and techniques. Repurposed wood speaks to sustainability, while the cabin's form references the vernacular wooden houses commonly seen in northern Thailand. Together these create a cabin that takes shape as a simple structure that is open to its surroundings to connect its inhabitants with nature.

WOOD AND MOUNTAIN CABIN (2021), Mae Rim, Chiang Mai, Thailand

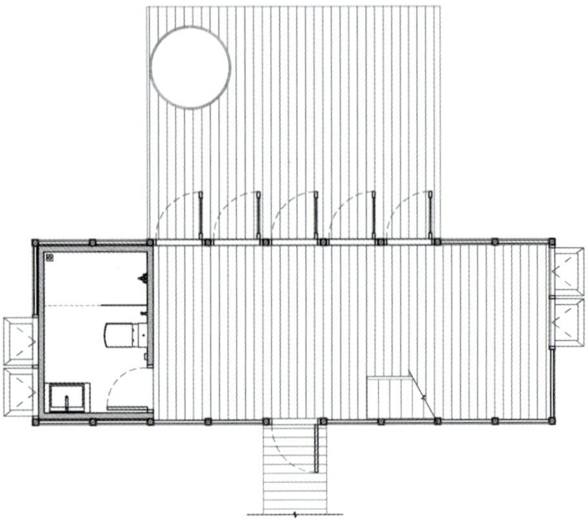

First-floor plan

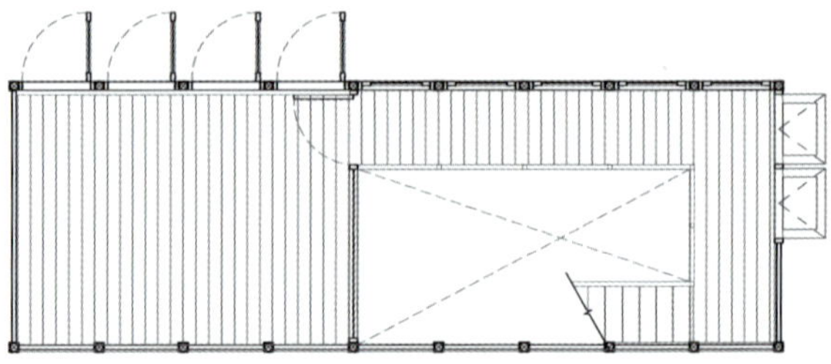

Second-floor plan

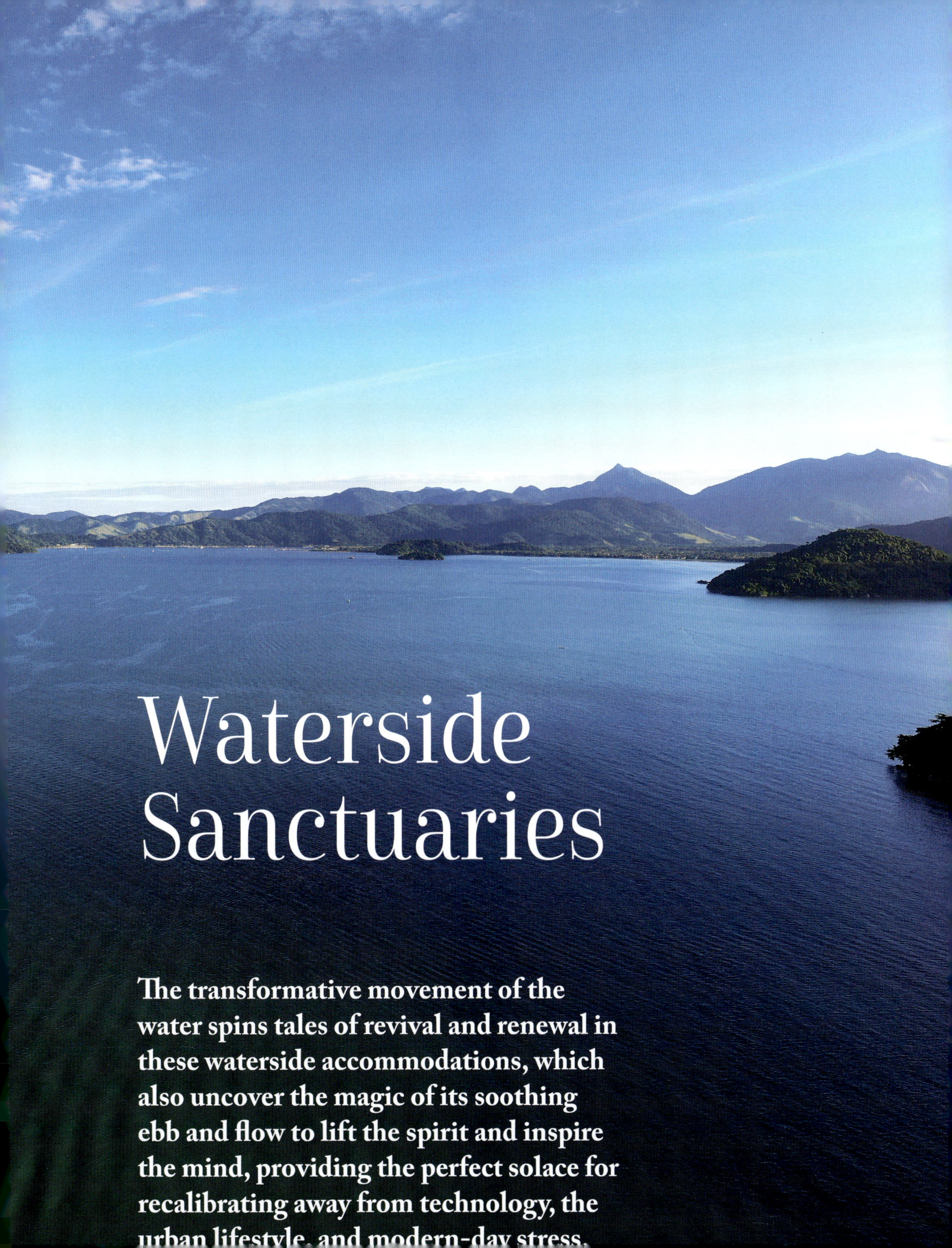

Waterside Sanctuaries

The transformative movement of the water spins tales of revival and renewal in these waterside accommodations, which also uncover the magic of its soothing ebb and flow to lift the spirit and inspire the mind, providing the perfect solace for recalibrating away from technology, the urban lifestyle, and modern-day stress.

Transforming Every Day

To truly experience nature is to live with the elements. This is the inspiration behind ANNA Stay, a dynamic wooden prefabricated house that can be flexibly assembled off-grid, or on. In the shape of an open platform, the structure plays with the configuration of its layers, so that its wooden exterior and glass interior can be customized to any occasion, mood, or weather.

Two different "shells" as outer walls are supported on rails, while the inner wall makes up a framework of wood and glass that is separated from the roofed wooden outer wall. Shifting the "shells" enables different unique set-ups.

A range of fitted amenities makes the cabin suitable for both long- or short-term occupancy. These include a kitchen, shower, toilet, and storage functions. A mezzanine above the kitchen even provides space for a second double bed, so that a family of four can comfortably enjoy the experience of the cabin. The cabin can be delivered as a flatpack, consisting of twenty-six parts and fourteen steel pillars measuring 4.9 feet (1.5 meters). Using a mini electric crane, the cabin can be built in seven days by five people, and disassembled in five.

Designed to encourage a deeper connection and interaction with nature, the cabin creates the freedom to navigate with your senses and live among the abundance of life, and be a part of everything around you.

ANNA STAY (2021), Schaijk, The Netherlands

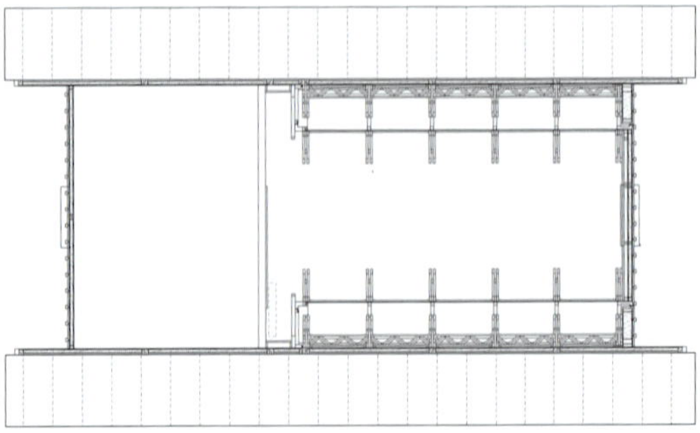

Mezzanine floor plan

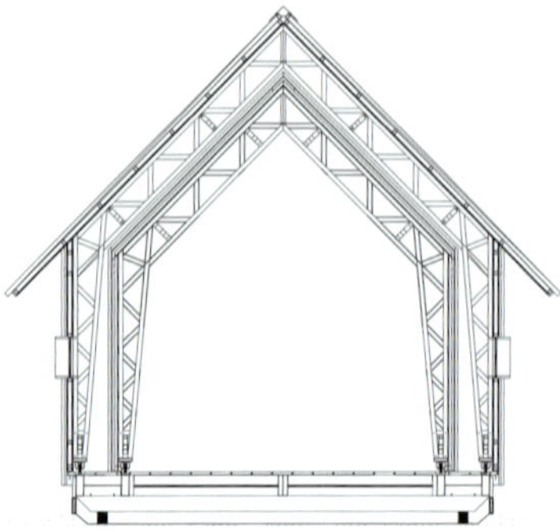

Section

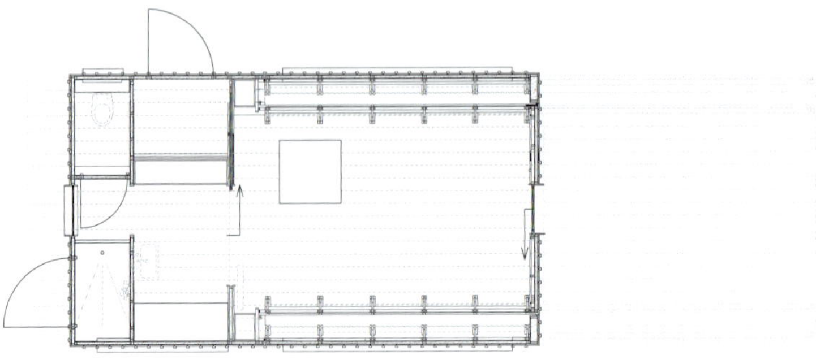

First-floor plan

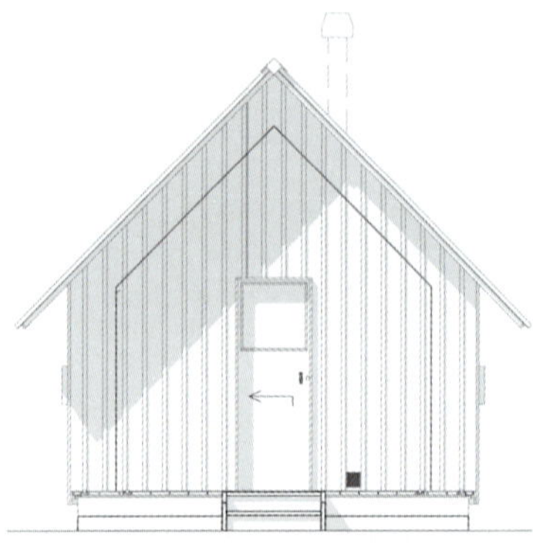

Elevation

Nature's Embrace

Sceneries of vibrant greens are set against vivid blues, and held in triangulated schemes as an ode to nature's most basic structural system: the triangle—a special organization in dynamic equilibrium, like the very character of Bow House.

Conceptualized as triangular modulations in different scales, this triangular volume iterates a treehouse typology and sits on extended pillars on Praia do Rosa beach in Paraty, Rio de Janeiro, Brazil, floating above a vibrant carpet of tropical greenery, on a steep waterfront terrain.

The triangular geometry redundancy on the floor plan and section, as well as on the tetrahedron roof system, promotes both structural and perceptive strategy. The cabin organizes a compact living space that is further modulated in sub-triangles to create repeating visual patterns in the space, as well as finishings, deploying matching aesthetic flourishes all around the cabin.

The main bedroom is arranged in the center, with the kitchen behind it, and the entrance and a bathroom are on side triangles. The terrace is set at the front and arranged in a point—in unison with the angles that guide the design scheme—to open like a ship bow to the sea. Around it, tree branches extend and interweave, wrapping the house in a leafy embrace.

As nature weaves its tale, specially designed décor accents tell the story of the locality—such as curtains made out of local shrimp fishing nets and wall lamps developed from traditional bronze boat drains—elevating the experience of the cabin and the landscape.

BOW HOUSE (2021), Paraty, Rio de Janeiro, Brazil

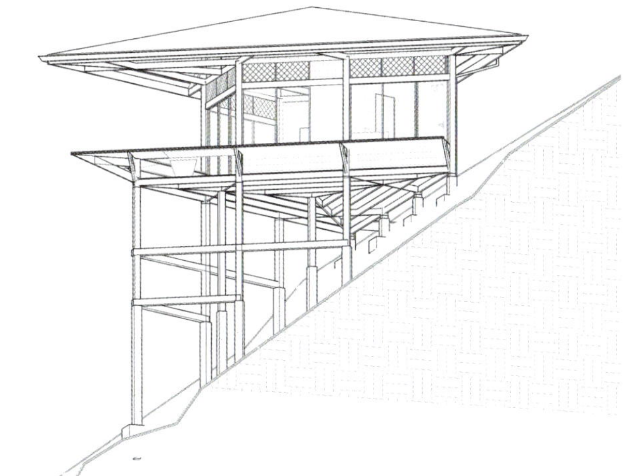

Elevation

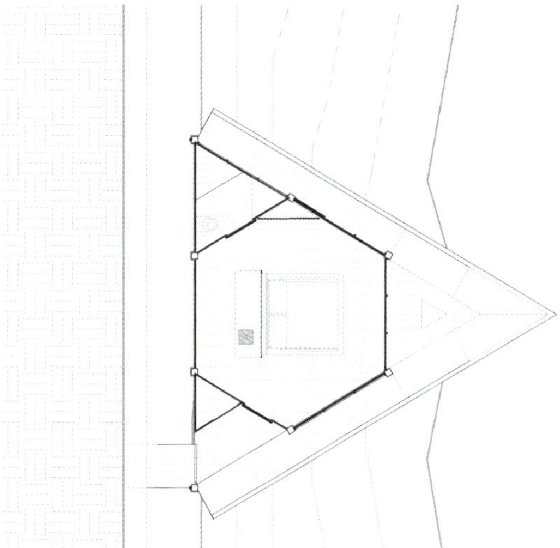

Floor plan

Fjordan Escape

Overlooking a view of hills that roll into the Norwegian fjord, Cabin Rones sits, as days pass in intimate connection with the landscape.

This minimalist cabin, located north of Trondheim, claims a steep, rough site that has both rocky outcrops and feathery grass. A compact footprint adapts the cabin to its landscape, while preserving the site and the wild nature that embraces it. The main floor is a concrete construction with three different levels that adapt to the terrain. The concrete base and the big wooden windows at the front support the second floor, expressed as a triangular volume in cross-laminated timber wrapped in black roofing felt.

The interior is mainly characterized by raw concrete walls, a polished concrete floor, wooden windows, and Norwegian pine, which iterates the second story. The furnishings, made out of Norwegian birch, help create a pale, placid interior that is offset by the deeper hues of the concrete floor. Matched to the tranquil vibe of the landscape, the mild décor seems to extend, even complete, the connection to the surroundings. Gutter components and other outdoor detailing are fashioned in untreated copper, so that they will darken with time, lending an aged patina that will blend with the hues of nature. With a back wall in concrete and a glass façade that greets the fjord, the cabin evokes a sheltering atmosphere in which one can reach out to nature, as it reaches out to us.

CABIN RONES (2018), Steinkjer, Norway

Section

A Sense of Mystique

This small, shingle-clad cabin built on the ruins of a stone foundation, on the shore of Lake Porovesi, central Finland, is an imaginative expression that rejects the current paradigm of Nordic architecture, intead drawing influences from the universe of '80s adventure movies.

Around a concept of baroque galore, mysticism, and multi-sensory experiences the cabin fools the eye to appear larger than its actual size, with its small tar-coated shingle exterior cladding. This, in turn, makes the surrounding landscape more impactful. Material intensity on the exterior is intentionally matched with the landscape to help the building blend into the surroundings and shadows.

The plan features a basilica-shaped workspace, side aisles, and a high-ceiling main nave. The walls and the arched ceiling are clad with dark oak boarding, and the floor is paved with rough stone slabs, reminiscent of an old church. The dark oak cladding on the surfaces of the high main nave creates a sensation of mystical darkness. Above the secondary functions in the eastern end of the main space is a small mezzanine accessed by a dark oak ladder, where a circular window catches the rays of the sunrise. The functions in the side aisles are integrated into the fixtures—on one, there is a worktable made of oak and a cast iron fireplace, and on the other, there is an oak bookshelf. From the floor to the tabletop, all fixtures are in light-hued oak, creating a fluid, seamless palette.

THE FILMMAKER'S HUT (2020), Iisalmi, Finland

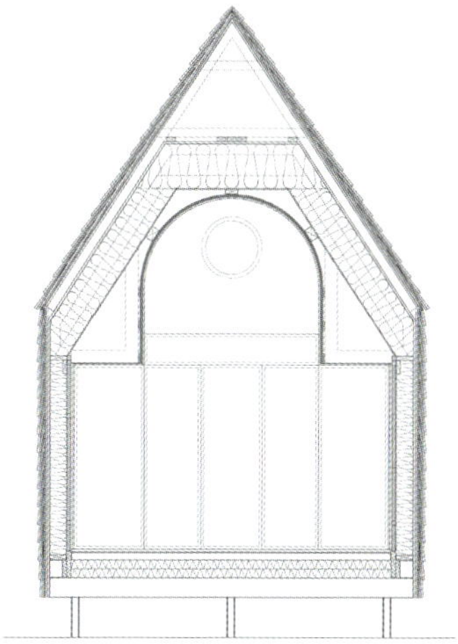

Cross section

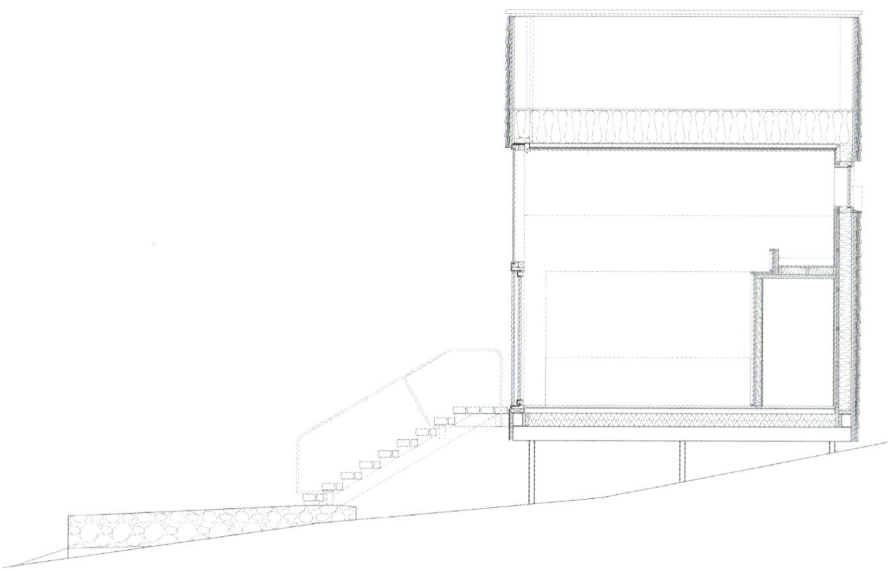

Long section

Wild and Free

This cabin is designed to be placed in the most isolated of locations and "disappear" as far off the grid as possible. This spirit of adventure lies in a convenient, prefabricated assembly model, with energy storage, and a wastewater treatment system. The cabin is scalable, transportable, and can be dismantled and moved to new sites.

The concept is driven by the need to radically rethink and minimize ecological impact on the environment, and to illustrate how small-scale architecture and small-scale technology can replace big volumes and centralized grid systems, even in future housing solutions. Inspired by life in the Finnish archipelago—framed by traditional habitats, small buildings, and living in harmony with nature—the cabin constitutes a light infrastructure to reduce pre-construction work that could damage the environment.

The wooden cabin can be assembled without heavy construction equipment, allowing it to be installed in extremely isolated locations. Its scalability also allows multiple units to be joined to create a larger cabin. The cabin's water autonomy is based on the collection of rainwater and gray water filtered by a purification system. This system operates in a closed circuit, where all gray water is collected and recycled, without discharging any into nature; the waste from the dry toilet is composted and reused as fertilizer. Solar panels and a fuel cell provide power for amenities that include a light, refrigerator, microwave, television, and even air conditioning.

MAJAMAJA WUORIO OFF-GRID CABIN (2020), Helsinki, Finland

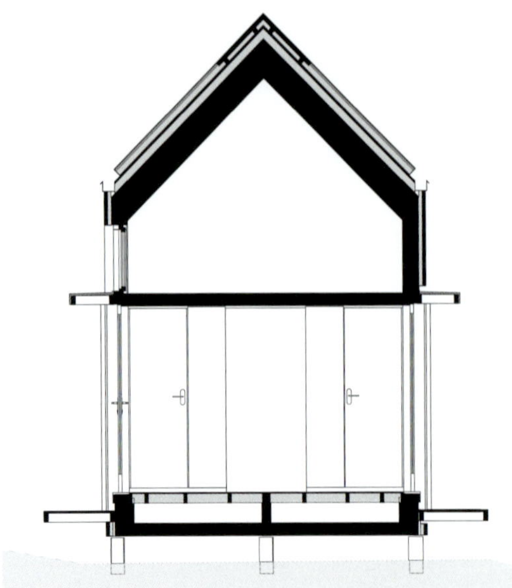

Cross section

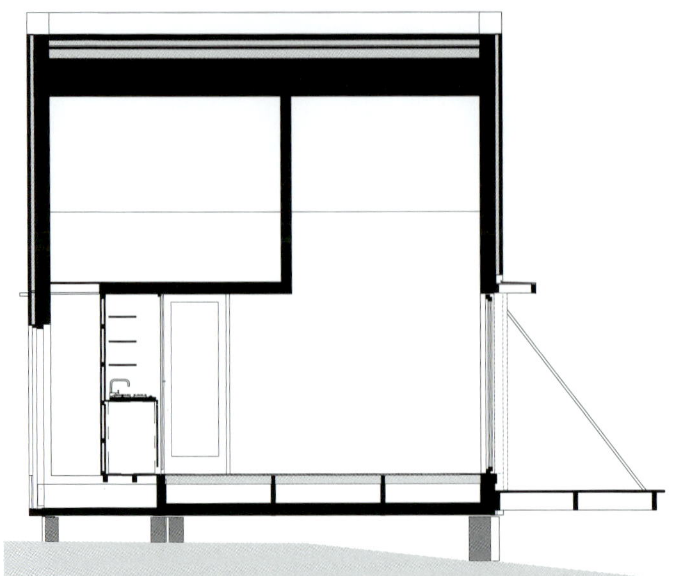

Long section

Ö is for Island

This island retreat is the realization of a dream—of a husband-and-wife design team, built on summers boating in the Finnish Archipelago. Project Ö—"Ö" meaning "island" in Swedish—is located on a private island on the edge of Archipelago National Park; it has a small pine forest to the south and dramatic rocky bays on the north.

Gable roofs pay tribute to the traditional Finnish archipelago vernacular and tree logs (easy to transport and assemble) form the walls. Logs do not require insulation, allowing moisture to travel freely, and keeping the structure healthy. They are kept bare in the interior, treated simply with oil to prevent yellowing over time; on the outside, they are clad in thermo pine. All other exterior wood surfaces are also made of thermo pine, which is excellent for its stability and durability.

Spaces are designed to be compact without compromising functionality and comfort. Large windows maximize views from within, while a narrow plan allows public and private functions to be spaced further apart—the sauna, bathroom, and toilet are at one end, and the living area, kitchen, and bedroom are at the other. In between, there is a sheltered outdoor space with an outdoor kitchen and dining area. The self-sufficient cabin uses solar power for energy and filtered seawater for drinking water, and is equipped with running water, a flush toilet, and heating and cooling. Hot running water is produced with a sauna stove and the same system provides heat to the floors.

PROJECT Ö (2018), Archipelago National Park, Finland

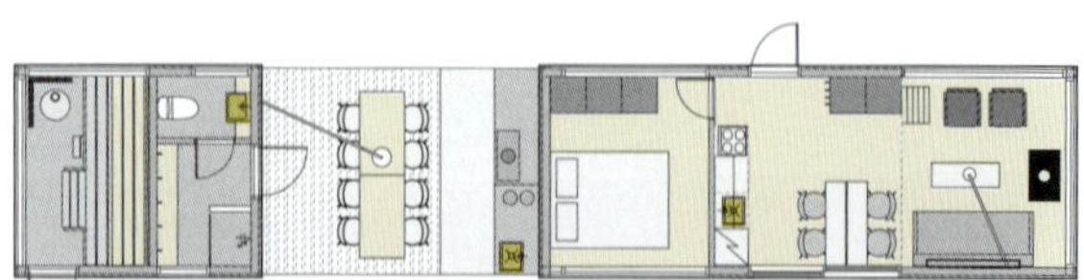

Cabin floor plan

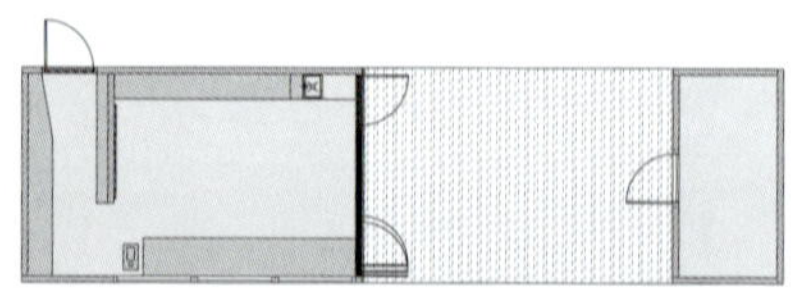

Workshop floor plan

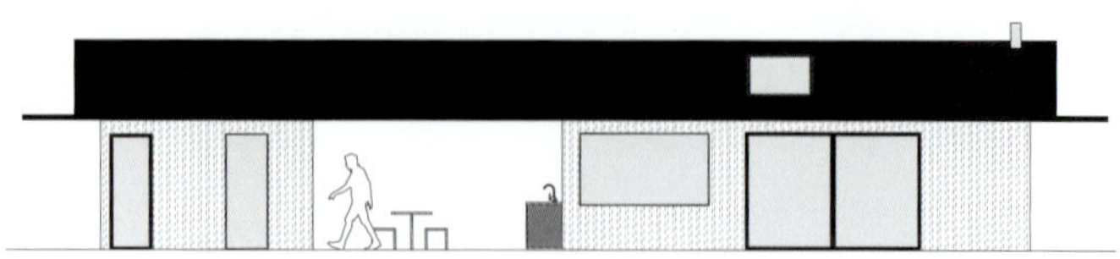

Cabin west elevation

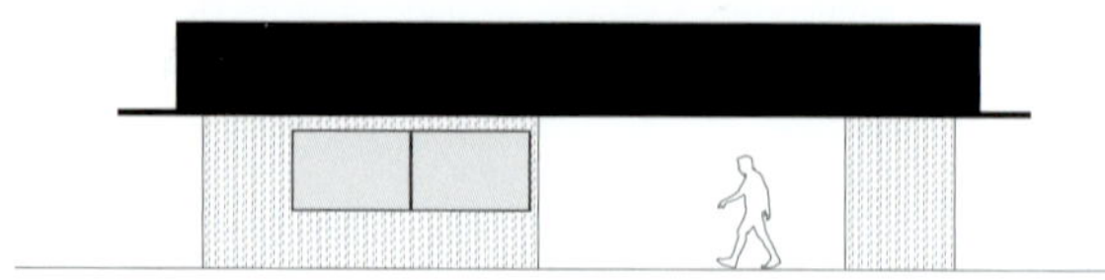

Workshop west elevation

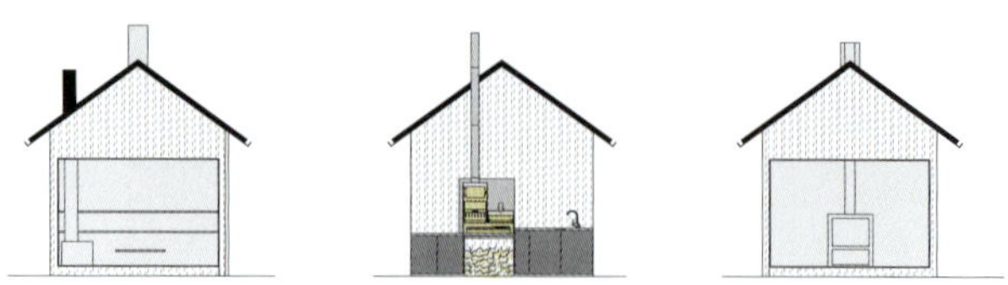

Cabin: north elevation; north section; south elevation

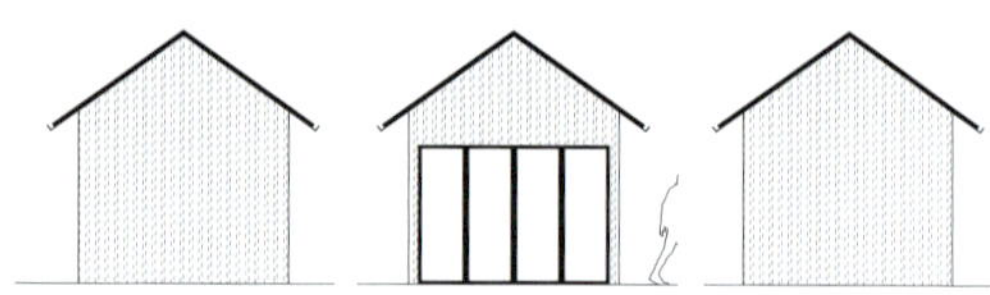

Workshop: north elevation; south section; south elevation

Riverside Views

This in-campus shelter for a university professor, located on the banks of the Calle-Calle River in Valvidia, Región de Los Ríos, Chile, is built compact, in order to support its limited site and size. The architecture is drawn in, focusing on itself as a way to mediate the harsh southern climate, yet still generates exchanges with the outside through a window that looks out to the river. The elongated form is arranged perpendicular to the river to refrain from blocking the views of the buildings around it, and also to frame the riverscape scenery.

A sector of the cabin is elevated to create a space of greater height internally. In this way, the open plan of the cabin, selected to extend some amplitude to the tight program, is reformulated by a key central element: the stands—which limit the traditional free floor, but make room for a wide range of other possibilities. These differing interior levels, therefore, become both the living room and the seating for the dining table, in addition to functioning as a transitional space.

The visual escape of the volume is planned at the rear and achieved through a large curtain wall; the desk and bed are located in this section. This space faces the river directly in a singular way. The elevated condition of this sector shortens the range between the river and the cabin, making the distance to the river visually disappear, while also generating a novel visual horizon for the user.

RIVERSIDE CABIN (2019). Valdivia, Región de Los Ríos, Chile

Section

Letting in the Light

Each day begins looking up (literally!) in this sleek glass and steel cabin that bestows unrestricted views of drifting clouds in the day and glittering stars at night. With a glass ceiling and glass walls, the cabin hides nothing of its surroundings—around and above—and takes the description "immersive" to a whole new level, or "sky-high."

The unit is delivered ready-to-use to the site, where it is connected to infrastructure and installed on foundations built according to the manufacturer's instructions. The modular design allows it to be easily adapted to a variety of functions.

A mirror-like glass exterior renders a delicate reflection of the surroundings, artfully dissolving the cabin into the landscape, so its occupants can fuse with the landscape, as a part of it. This expressive, sleek exterior extends fluidly, interrupted only by the black seams of the glazing system and the black perimeter of the steel floor plate. In this cabin, the surroundings blend with the interior, and the interior blends with the surroundings, such that the most prominent aspect of the interior décor is the exterior itself, arranging scenes of the surrounding landscape as the main interior finish. The triangular shapes of the steel structures are oriented to capture the widest view possible of the nature on the site, with as little obstruction as possible. Lighting is integrated in this steel beam structure and cleverly uses the glass surfaces as a reflective backdrop to create interesting multidimensionality within the space.

SMART LUCIA (2019), Iisalmi, Finland

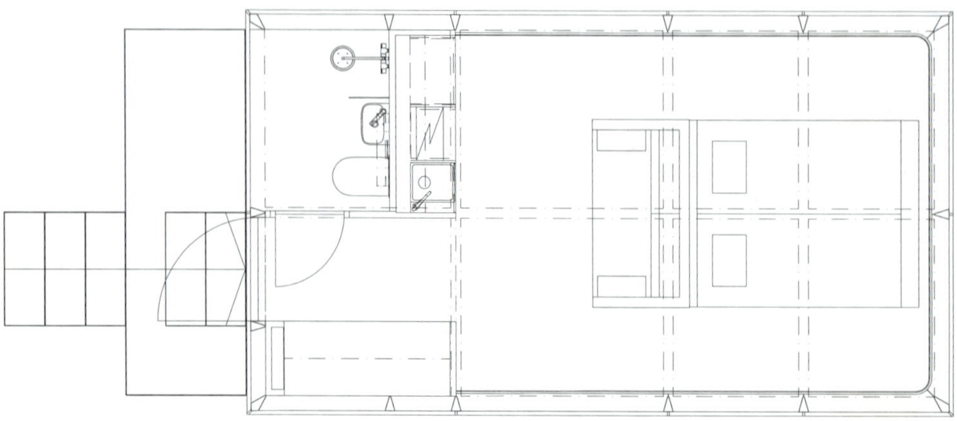

Floor plan

PROJECT CREDITS

14–19 **SITTING PRETTY**
019 Cabin | ŠA atelier || sarkauskai.com
LOCATION Apple Island, Lithuania
COMPLETED 2020
AREA 247.6 ft^2 (23 m^2)
PHOTOGRAPHY Vaidotas Darulis

20–23 **NOTHING TO WASTE**
Ashen Cabin | HANNAH || hannah-office.org
LOCATION Ithaca, New York, United States
COMPLETED 2019
AREA 107.6 ft^2 (10 m^2)
PHOTOGRAPHY Andy Chen

24–27 **FLOATING HIDEAWAY**
Cabin Moss | Béres Architects || beresattila.hu
LOCATION Kőszeg, Hungary
COMPLETED 2021
AREA 430.6 ft^2 (40 m^2)
PHOTOGRAPHY Tamás Bujnovszky

28–35 **PERCHED FOR THE VIEW**
Cabin on a Rock | I-Kanda Architects || i-kanda.com
LOCATION White Mountains, New Hampshire, United States
COMPLETED 2017
AREA 900 ft^2 (84 m^2)
PHOTOGRAPHY Matt Delphenich

36–43 **A WOVEN DREAM**
Casa Tejida (Woven House) | Santiago Pradilla, Zuloark || zuloark.com
LOCATION Cundinamarca, Colombia
COMPLETED 2019
Area 1,291.7 ft^2 (120 m^2)
PHOTOGRAPHY Federico Cairoli

44–49 **PEACEFUL REFLECTIONS**
Forest Glamp | Bourgeois / Lechasseur architectes || bourgeoislechasseur.com
LOCATION Québec, Canada
COMPLETED 2021
AREA 861.1 ft^2 (80 m^2)
PHOTOGRAPHY Adrien Williams, Maxime Brouillet

50–57 **SIMPLICITY FOR EFFECT**
Huaira | Diana Salvador & Javier Mera || huaira.ec
LOCATION Puerto Quito, Ecuador
COMPLETED 2019
AREA 430.6 ft^2 (16 m^2)
PHOTOGRAPHY JAG Studio

58–65 **CANDLE IN THE WOODS**
Kynttilä | Ortraum || ortraum.com
LOCATION Lake Saimaa, Finland
COMPLETED 2020
AREA 170 ft^2 (16 m^2)
PHOTOGRAPHY Marc Goodwin / Archmospheres

66–71 **SWAMP SERENITY**
Maidla Nature Villa | b210 architects || b210.ee
LOCATION Rapla County, Estonia
COMPLETED 2020
AREA 301 ft^2 (28 m^2)
PHOTOGRAPHY Tõnu Tunnel

72–77 **UP IN THE AIR**
Niliaitta | Studio Puisto Architects Ltd || studiopuisto.fi
LOCATION Kivijärvi, Finland
COMPLETED 2020
AREA 387.5 ft^2 (36 m^2)
PHOTOGRAPHY Marc Goodwin / Archmospheres

78–83 **COUNTRY CHARM**
Oak Cabin | Out of the Valley || outofthevalley.co.uk
LOCATION Devon, United Kingdom
COMPLETED 2017
AREA 258.3 ft^2 (24 m^2)
PHOTOGRAPHY Rupert McKelvie

84–91 **COMING HOME**
Space of Mind | Studio Puisto Architects Ltd || studiopuisto.fi
LOCATION Porvoo, Finland
COMPLETED 2020
AREA 107.6 ft^2 (10 m^2)
PHOTOGRAPHY Marc Goodwin / Archmospheres

92–99 **NATURE'S NEST**
Woodnest | Helen & Hard || helenhard.no
LOCATION Odda, Norway
COMPLETED 2020
AREA 161.5 ft^2 (15 m^2)
PHOTOGRAPHY Sindre Ellingsen

102–9 **THE EDGE OF TRANSCENDENCE**
Bivouac Fanton | Demogo || demogo.it
LOCATION Dolomites (Belluno), Italy
COMPLETED 2021
AREA 322.9 ft^2 (30 m^2)
PHOTOGRAPHY Iwan Baan

110–13 **A SENSITIVE SOLUTION**
Cabin A24 | Dev Desai Architects Associates (DDAA) || ddaa.in
LOCATION Coorg, India
COMPLETED 2021
AREA 225 ft^2 (20.9 m^2)
PHOTOGRAPHY Kunal Daswani

114–21 **ARCTIC OUTLOOKS**
Hammerfest Hiking Cabins | SPINN Arkitekter || www.spinnark.no
LOCATION Hammerfest, Norway
COMPLETED 2019
AREA 161.5 ft^2 (15 m^2)
PHOTOGRAPHY Tor Even Mathisen

122–27 **REFUGE FOR REFLECTION**
Mountaineer's Refuge | Gonzalo Iturriaga Arquitectos || gonzaloiturriaga.cl
LOCATION Valparaíso región, Chile
COMPLETED 2016
AREA 645.8 ft^2 (60 m^2)
PHOTOGRAPHY Federico Cairoli

128–35 **CABINS IN THE CLOUDS**
Tungestølen Hiking Cabins | Snøhetta || snohetta.com
LOCATION Luster, Norway
COMPLETED 2019
AREA 4,305.6 ft^2 (400 m^2)
PHOTOGRAPHY Jan M. Lillebø, Ketil Jacobsen

138–45 **ISLAND IDEALS**
Bruny Island Hideaway | Maguire + Devine Architects || maguiredevine.com.au
LOCATION Bruny Island, Tasmania, Australia
COMPLETED 2017
AREA 301.4 ft^2 (28 m^2)
PHOTOGRAPHY Rob Maver

Published in Australia in 2022 by
The Images Publishing Group Pty Ltd
ABN 89 059 734 431

OFFICES

Melbourne
Waterman Business Centre
Suite 64, Level 2 UL40
1341 Dandenong Road
Chadstone, VIC 3148
Australia
Tel: +61 3 8564 8122

New York
6 West 18th Street 4B
New York, NY 10011
United States
Tel: +1 212 645 1111

Shanghai
6F, Building C,
838 Guangji Road
Hongkou District,
Shanghai 200434
China
Tel: +86 021 31260822

books@imagespublishing.com
www.imagespublishing.com

All photography is attributed in the Project Credits on pages 262–63, with the following exceptions: Pages 2–3: Tor Even Mathisen (SPINN Arkitekter, Hammerfest Hiking Cabins); page 4: Iwan Baan (Demogo, Bivouac Fanton); page 6: Federico Cairoli (Santiago Pradilla, Zuloark, Casa Tejida [Woven House]); page 9: Jan M. Lillebø (Snøhetta, Tungestølen Hiking Cabins); page 10: Marc Goodwin / Archmospheres (Pirinen Salo Oy, The Filmmaker's Hut); pages 12–13: Marc Goodwin / Archmospheres (Studio Puisto Architects Ltd, Space of Mind); pages 100–101: Ketil Jacobsen (Snøhetta, Tungestølen Hiking Cabins); pages 136–37: Rupert McKelvie (Out of the Valley, Holly Water Cabin); pages 210–11: Rafael Medeiros (Atelier Marko Brajovic, Bow House)

NATIONAL LIBRARY OF AUSTRALIA

A catalogue record for this book is available from the National Library of Australia

Title: Modern Cabins: Return to the Wild
Author: Dev Desai (Introduction)
ISBN: 9781864709315

FSC www.fsc.org MIX Paper from responsible sources FSC® C106600

Printed and bound by DZS GRAFIK (Slovenia) on 150gsm Galerie Art Silk paper

IMAGES has included on its website a page for special notices in relation to this and its other publications. Please visit www.imagespublishing.com